A Manual for Teaching English in China

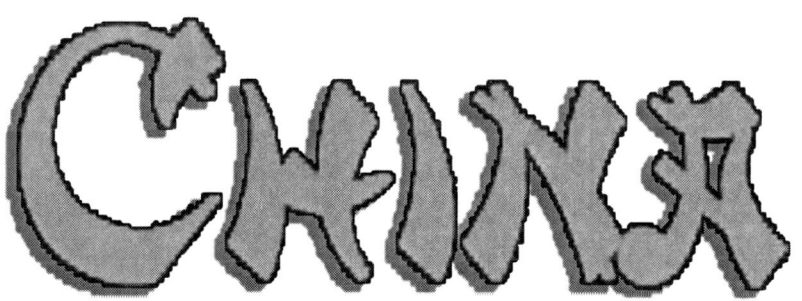

This manual can be used in any ESL class in the world.

Bill Burkett

© 2009 Bill Burkett
All Rights Reserved.

No part of this publication may be reproduced, stored in a retrieval system, or transmitted, in any form or by any means, electronic, mechanical, photocopying, recording, or otherwise, without the written permission of the author.

First published by Dog Ear Publishing
4010 W. 86th Street, Ste H
Indianapolis, IN 46268
www.dogearpublishing.net

ISBN: 978-159858-916-0

This book is printed on acid-free paper.

Printed in the United States of America

Dedication

I dedicate this manual of practical teaching methods to the real heroes of China's English literacy, the Chinese teachers of English. They stand in the remote classrooms of China's countryside and the modern schoolrooms of large cities, often living sacrificially to mold young lives. This commitment to their profession launches their students into a more prosperous future because they have given them the English language, the business language of the world. The students they have taught come to us, the foreign English teachers, to colleges and universities across China, reading, writing and speaking English. These teachers who prepared these students are the unsung heroes of English literacy that have made a great contribution to China's economic future. They have nurtured the World Trade Organization – WTO – generation of The New China. If you are Chinese and you can read these lines, you have a Chinese teacher to thank.

Contents

Dedication iii

Preface vii

Chapter 1 1
Your First Steps Toward Teaching in China

Chapter 2 12
Understanding Your Students

Chapter 3 24
The Central Goal of the Oral English Program

Chapter 4 33
Basic Class Structures

Chapter 5 42
Documentation: A Source of Order in the Classroom

Chapter 6 50
Behavior and Decorum

Chapter 7 57
Read Along

Chapter 8 69
Talk Along and Follow Along

Chapter 9 73
Secondary Objectives and Miscellaneous Exercises

Chapter 10 83
Correcting Chronic Mispronunciations

Chapter 11 99
Teaching the *Whole* Student

Chapter 12 109
English Corner: The Classroom Without Walls

Chapter 13 115
An Introduction to Grading Oral English

Chapter 14 124
Exam Basics

Chapter 15 132
The Oral Exam

Chapter 16 147
Tips for Administering the Oral Exam

Chapter 17 162
Scoring Methods for the Oral Exam

Chapter 18 168
Double-checking the Accuracy of Your Oral Scoring

Chapter 19 175
Teaching Resources and Class Materials

Chapter 20 183
Living in China

Textual Initialisms and Glossary 190

Preface

Imagine this scenario: You are finally boarding your flight to China with about thirteen hours of flying time ahead of you before landing at your destination. As you settle down in your seat, waiting for the drinks to come down the aisle, you start wondering again what in the world teaching English in China will be like, anyway? You're struggling with how you'll approach this new teaching job when you begin your classes. A hundred questions form in your mind, and your anxiety level begins to rise. Suddenly the man sitting next to you strikes up a conversation about the weather and other small talk. Then he tells you that he lives in China, has been working as a teacher there for seven years, and really loves it! He is now returning to teach at a University in Chengdu. You can hardly believe your ears! Here is a teacher who has been teaching English in China sitting right beside you. You have a captive source of information for the long flight over the Pacific Ocean! You don't want to scare him, so you very casually tell him you're going to China for your first time as a teacher, and you have no idea how you will approach this new job. Being the dedicated teacher he is, he offers to answer any questions you have. Now, pretend these events have happened to you, and that I am that man sitting next to you. By the time you land in China, you will feel a lot better about your new job. So, buckle up your seat belt, settle back, and relax as I try to answer all of the major questions you may have. And, by the way, what we'll be talking about will help new Chinese teachers of English as well.

When one undertakes to write a manual, small or large, it usually indicates that the writer wants to share information that he feels is not out there for the people who need it. Such a manual should provide special information that's needed but not available in one source. This is the case with this manual, in which I endeavor to help young aspiring Chinese and foreign teachers to enter their classroom with a better sense of direction than if they had not had the help it offers. Academics are essential to the progress of any society, but too often practical advice and classroom savvy are lacking. You may feel well taught in your field of expertise, but you soon learn upon entering the classroom, that you still have a lot of practical procedures you feel a little vague and uncertain about, and especially, as it applies to Oral English. This little easy reference manual, *Teaching English in China – TEC,* will hopefully supplement what you already know with some good, practical principles in classroom procedures.

I have a very high level of respect for all of my Chinese colleagues who, by their teaching efforts, are developing young lives into useful adults who will go on to build the new China in the WTO generation. Teachers who can release each student at the end of the year knowing they have made a positive contribution to that student's future represent the greatest hope for China's future. Young people educated in the English language have a better chance of knowing a higher quality of life. This *TEC Manual* is intended to be a primer to enhance any English teacher's ability to better build these young lives. The reward of being a good teacher is the satisfaction of knowing you have put into the world new adult people who are not a part of the world's problems, but rather, are a part of the solution to those problems.

For the new Oral English foreign teachers arriving from abroad, this manual offers good information and many teaching methods that you can use to better organize and conduct your classes. Indeed, if I were to give this manual a key word, it would be the word *practical*. For students who are preparing to teach upon graduation from college, this manual is packed with practical information that you will never learn in the college classroom, unless your college has made this manual required reading. Seasoned teachers who have long experience in teaching will also benefit from many of the tips given here regarding achieving good pronunciation and understanding the language hurdles that make some words too high to get over. I have lectured middle school teachers and found many of these seasoned teachers were teaching incorrect pronunciation to their middle school students. Many aspects of this practical manual on teaching English will help even the older and more experienced English teachers. Teaching is an art that can constantly be refined and brought to new levels of effectiveness.

This *TEC* manual is directed to all those involved in learning and teaching English, but even teachers who teach other subjects will find methods and class structure ideas here that will help them. If you are a foreign teacher coming to China, this little manual will give you a valuable glimpse into the classroom of an experienced foreign teacher in a Chinese middle school, college, or university setting, beginning with the very first day. Of course, this information will help you get started and introduce you to what to expect. This is a primer, not an exhaustive authority on Oral English procedures. It also gives you a good idea of the range of issues that can be involved in teaching Oral English. You will, in time, develop your own proficient methods of teaching according to your personality, your formal training background, and your personal teaching philosophies as you progress in your career teaching in China.

I remember very well my first Oral English class. I had no idea what to do, and in the third class after my arrival, I was still floundering. I will never forget the day that the president of the school came to sit in on my lesson! I didn't even know what I was doing, and here was the president, sitting back at the rear of the room, arms folded looking at me askance. Sweating a little, I decided to deliver a lecture on the subject of time, explaining that time was like money, because you could purchase things in life with time. However, if you spent it wisely, you could purchase things with time that you could not with money. As I lectured, I stopped along the way to emphasize pronunciation and new words. The president became so excited about the lecture that he ordered all of the English teachers on the staff (fifty of them) to attend my classes when they did not have their own classes! Now I was really in hot water! I had to produce miracles in every class or risk jeopardizing my image. Perhaps it was that pressure that made me press ahead for results with my class.

I had taught in many different kinds of teaching environments over the years, but when I came to China, I didn't have the slightest idea what materials would be available to me or even what textbooks I would be using. I was especially in the dark about classroom procedures and methods, not to mention the grading system. What was going to be expected of me as a teacher of Oral English? I did everything I could to find the practical information I needed. I found some information scattered across several very good ESL websites, but nothing that provided step-by-step classroom procedures. It was then that the idea was born in my mind to write such a practical manual that would take a teacher by the hand and lead him or her through the first few days and weeks of teaching Oral English in a Chinese classroom. I also had a good friend teaching in China who helped me tremendously, but Floyd wasn't there to help me in my classroom. A practical manual to help me just wasn't out there. Well, I am happy to say that it *is* out there now!

I am not implying that you should follow every piece of advice found here. Rather, I am setting forth some vital information to help you in the areas of teaching that you will encounter as you move through your first semester. You will meet and discuss teaching with your many new colleagues, and they too will share with you some excellent ideas that you will surely want to consider using. This manual probably contains more information than you will be able to use, but it is a rich source of practical ideas from which you can choose when you are just starting out.

I am fully aware that the teaching procedures set down in this manual represent my personal approach to teaching and will differ from the procedures of other teachers with perhaps much more experience. Teaching a language class is new to most of us when we come to China. I want to provide teachers not only with methods of teaching, but also with some special helpful advice to help the foreign teacher adjust to the culture of China.

There are manuals out there that are very good and much more thoroughly written by professionals, but they are mainly available through the placement agencies that train their candidates for teaching abroad. Most of these manuals are quite large and generic in their approach, written for any foreign country and not for China in particular. This manual is written only with teaching in China in mind.

If you are coming to China as a foreign teacher to teach Oral English at the college level, you will find that your students will have five to seven years of English when they come into your class. They have been taught by deeply committed Chinese teachers. In their other Chinese/English classes, your students are learning grammar, reading, writing skills and composition. In addition, speech, memorization and workbooks have all been a part of their other English classes under the Chinese teachers. Most students can read and write English with much more proficiency than they can speak it. This is certainly one of the reasons why the Chinese government saw the need to raise the English (and other foreign language) speech skills to match the reading and writing skills, of which the average student seems to have the better command.

Foreign teachers are to provide the Chinese students with something the Chinese teachers cannot give them, and that is the opportunity to speak with foreign teachers and learn to improve their pronunciation of English. The exposure of the students to pure native English is the correct special emphasis of the Oral English classes. The Chinese Department of Education spends millions of renminbi, or RMB, each month to pay the travel and monthly salaries of foreign teachers so that our Chinese students may have the special privilege of being exposed to the sound of pure English speech. Forgive me for repeating this job description so many times in different ways throughout this manual, but it is extremely important to have that singular purpose imbedded in our minds every time we enter a classroom.

Some strong advice for the foreign teacher: When you come to China, you will see that the social habits here are much different than in the West. Family ties are stronger; there is a deeper respect for symbols of authority including teachers and especially parents, and for the Chinese authorities and Chinese tradition. College freshmen are bonded to their grandparents with the same affection as for their parents. On any given night, you will see grandparents out with their grandchildren. I have seen as many children with their grandparents as I have with their parents. You should note all of these features of Chinese culture, and then adjust your teaching, and even your lifestyle, to complement and enhance these positive cultural traits, and not defy or be secretly set on changing them to your cultural values.

As a foreign teacher, I urge you to leave cultural philosophies peculiar to the West behind you, and to open your mind to new ways of seeing the world. It's not advisable to impose your cultural habits on the Chinese. There is already enough corrupting influence coming into China from the West through the film and video industry. The tendency of some of us to think we do it better where we come from really just represents a difference in habit and cultural perception. The way in which we are accustomed to viewing the world is not necessarily the better way. The old idiom, *When in Rome, do as the Romans do,* is good advice when you come here. In my experience, having resided both in China for seven years and the United States, and having lived in forty-three other countries in less than fifty years, the Chinese traditional culture is one of the most highly civilized in the world.

The Chinese student is very patriotic and loves his Motherland. To make this point meaningful, I will be very blunt with any foreign colleagues who are reading these lines. Historically,

Western countries have ravaged this land and the people of China since the time of Marco Polo. This was possible partly because the Chinese people are strong but gracious in nature. However, since the revolution and the bonding of the fifty-six ethnic peoples that make up China, there is a silent but deep-rooted resolve in their natures never to be pushed around by foreign powers again. Foreign teachers must respect that historical fact and respect the laws of the People's Republic of China when they arrive. We who come from the West should carefully observe the Chinese behavior. We could learn a lot from it. You will not be in China long before you see that you are destined to have a wonderful experience and meet some extremely nice people who will be among your dearest friends.

Chapter One
The First Steps Toward Teaching in China

Finding your job in China should not prove too difficult a challenge. If anyone in your family or circle of friends has taught in China, then that is where you should begin. If these contacts are in China when you become interested, then you should contact them. If they are able to help you make contact with a school near them, they would be the ideal contact. Then after being in China the first year, you could learn your way around and know better what you want in a school for the next contract.

The best way to establish yourself in China as a good teacher is to find the school setting that fits your preferences and then settle on that campus and faithfully and loyally serve that school. In this way, you establish yourself and become an asset to that school. On the other hand, some teachers prefer to change teaching locations from year to year and remain in China with seemingly good results.

Another way to know if China is where you want to teach is to visit China on a tourist visa; visit different campuses in a large city or two, and speak to different college and university officials about coming to China as a teacher. In this way, you could look over the facilities provided for foreign teachers and gain first hand knowledge of what's available and what your experience might be like. You would then return home and apply to the school of your choice. Of course, it's much less expensive to negotiate everything through e-mail, and that works well for many teaching candidates. Chinese school officials are very candid and honest when communicating with you long distance, via telephone or e-mail.

Do you prefer to work in a large and more Westernized part of China? Then you should choose the coastal cities such as Hong Kong, Shenzhen, Guangzhou and Shanghai. These regions pay more, but the cost of living is higher than in inland China.

Your level of education must be considered also. To teach in a college or university, you will need at least a bachelor's degree. If you are a high school graduate, you may qualify to teach in some middle schools (junior and senior high school students). Teachers are needed in high schools as well as in the colleges and universities, but if you sign with a middle school, be very sure that they are qualified to use foreign teachers before you spend a lot of time and money talking to them. All schools want foreign teachers badly. It sometimes happens that a school will invite a foreign teacher to come and teach in their school simply on a visitor's visa. This is illegal. To live and teach in China, you must have a Z visa, and that can only be procured with a yellow letter of invitation from the provincial government who issues this letter to the college. The college, in turn, will send this yellow letter to you to accompany your Z visa application.

After choosing and communicating with the school in which you want to work, you will send them a copy of your resume and a letter of intent, informing them of your desire to teach at their school. You will also need two or three letters of recommendation from people who know you well. The school will then send you a list of documents you must submit to them and a copy of the contract. Read it carefully. If you have any questions, you should discuss them by e-mail with the school. You should be clear on all the details of the arrangement, and keep these e-mail exchanges for future reference. The school officials will be eager to answer any questions you might have, and you can be assured that they will do this truthfully. You will not have to worry about Chinese authorities, especially in the state colleges and universities, leaving you with any false impressions. They are often honest to their own detriment. Once you understand everything, you can sign the contract and return it to the school with the other items they request to be sent. This may include a copy of your diploma, a couple of passport size photos for their files, and a copy of your passport, along with the letters of recommendation. Be very careful to submit all information honestly and accurately. The school, college, or university will process your contract application through the Provincial Foreign Affairs authorities.

When the Provincial Foreign Affairs Office – FAO – approves your application, the college will be given the official letter of invitation by them, and they will in turn mail that official document (invitation) to you. It is a large yellow paper. When you have that yellow letter in your hands, you then know that your invitation is finalized, and you have been approved to live and work in China. Not all schools are approved by the Chinese government to hire foreign teachers, but that official yellow letter proves that the school you have been talking to is authorized to hire foreign teachers. The provincial letter of invitation is only issued to schools with foreign teacher status. You cannot get a Z visa without that provincial letter of invitation. NEVER strike out to work in China with anything but a Z visa!

Once you have received that plain looking yellow letter of invitation from the college with whom you have contracted, you then send your passport with photos, visa application, and fees *with that official letter* to the Chinese embassy and apply for the Z visa. The Z visa is a working visa and permits you to live in China and receive pay here. Now you know the proper procedure for arranging a teaching position in China.

A word about physical examinations: If you contract for one year or less, you do NOT have to have a physical as of this writing. If you will be staying in China for more than one year, you will need to have a physical exam. If the school in which you're going to work requires the physical, just go ahead and process the visa because the physical exam is not required by the Chinese embassy to get your Z visa. You can get a physical exam in the Chinese hospital near your college after you arrive. When you get to China, you can ascertain whether or not your school will require the physical. Taking the physical in China after you arrive will most likely be cheaper and more convenient than having it done in the West.

You can visit the Chinese embassy website – search "Chinese embassy" on Google – to read all requirements for a Z visa. The embassy website is the final authority on the physical exam, for example. You can also print out the visa application from the Chinese embassy website if the form is not readily available at the travel agency where you buy your air ticket to China. I advise you to visit the Chinese embassy website and compare all information there with what you read here and from other sources of information. The rules change from time to time and you must consult the embassy (website) to be sure you have the most current information when you apply.

I also suggest that you use the Internet to gain more information about teaching in China. Simply search the terms *ESL* and/or *Teaching English in China* on any search engine. Search engines that are popular and powerful are www.dogpile.com and www.google.com. You'll have more hits than you can possibly visit. That's all there is to it, and you'll have all the information you want at your fingertips.

When you start looking for a job overseas, you can either go through a placement service or negotiate your own contract directly by contacting the college or university and establishing your own dialogue with the FAO of that school. This is quite easy with e-mail. Here are a few things you might want to consider asking them, depending on your age and personal preferences. Remember that you can freely discuss any preferences you may have with the friendly people with whom you are negotiating at the school:

1. **The number of hours you would be teaching each week –** Sixteen hours is normal.

2. **Would your weekends be free?** You may want Saturday and Sunday off to travel or simply relax.

3. **Do they have a website address you can visit?** This can be a handy source of information and will give you a sense of the campus.

4. **Is your apartment on campus or off campus?** If it is off campus, you may have to walk or travel to get to class. Many colleges have faculty living quarters on campus.

5. **Does the college provide a bicycle or other transportation?** This is significant if there is a distance between your apartment and your classroom.

6. **What utilities does the school pay, and what utilities must the teacher pay out of his salary?** The school usually pays all utilities, except personal ones such as your telephone bill. They may allow you an allowance, meaning you must pay what's over a certain set amount. I seldom have to pay, and this includes computer time also.

7. **Does the college provide a computer?** Most colleges do provide foreign teachers with a desktop computer in their apartment.

8. **Ask them to describe the living quarters.** Which floor, hot water, tub or shower, toilet seat or squatty potty (an opening flush with the floor)?

9. **Is there heat in the winter?**

10. **Is there air conditioning in the hot season?** It does get hot.

11. **Is the school approved to have foreign teachers with Z visas?**

12. **Is travel expense paid to and from China?** If you sign a contract for at least one school year, the school usually pays this expense. If you sign a contract for only one semester (six months), you will usually have to pay one way, and they pay one way.

If you do not have a computer or access to e-mail, the college officials may be willing to negotiate the contract with you over the telephone. These questions are important to you, especially if you are talking to two or three schools. You need to be able to compare what kind of experience and compensation each school is offering. When you make your decision, they will send you a contract to sign and return with all of the conditions including pay. Once you get the contract and look it over, then you will have a few more questions. Contracts are basically the same from one school to another, because they are forms recommended by the state educational authorities. Thus, they should be relatively easy to compare. I did, however, receive a five-page contract from one school and an eleven-page contract from another. Though they use the same forms, some contracts are more simplified and others more detailed. You may ask the college you're talking to for a copy of a sample contract. They will be happy to e-mail or fax it to you.

Please note that you may make special verbal agreements with a school concerning some point, such as your schedule preference, that will not be written into the contract. You will not have to worry, because you will find that Chinese school officials will always keep their commitments. I have never had a school official renege on a verbal agreement. It has been my experience that their word is as good as gold. It would be good to have it in writing or in an e-mail letter, so that if they forget, you can show them what you discussed, but verbal agreements are always kept. You will find that when dealing with Chinese officials in the college system, you are dealing with very honest people.

If you choose to go through a placement agency, it will often provide you with a special course included in its fee. It sometimes offers crash courses in the language of the country in which you are going to teach. Knowing Chinese is not required to teach English in China because your students all come to you having had six to eight years of English. In a middle school they will have had four to five years of English. You will appreciate the wonderful job the Chinese teachers have done, and communication with your students should not pose a problem. When you negotiate a contract by contacting a college in China directly, you eliminate the "middleman." However, there are advantages to going through an agency. The agency will do all of the negotiating with the school for you and help you all the way to the airport and your arrival in China. They familiarize you with manuals and give you practical tips before you land in China. Perhaps this manual serves a similar service.

Many of us in China have negotiated our own contracts. The people in the college administrations you will work with when negotiating a contract are all very fine people and extremely gracious. Everything is negotiable when you are discussing a contract with the schools.

Salaries will vary depending upon which region of China your school is located in and the degree you hold. The developed cities have a higher cost of living, and therefore the pay is higher. The rate of pay also depends upon the hours you teach each week and sometimes the degree you hold. A doctorate or master's degree is highly desirable because it raises the academic standard of the college. Specialized English teachers in such areas as law or medicine are usually paid more because the vocabulary demands special knowledge and skill. The State Foreign Affairs Office sets the pay rates. This is usually based upon a sixteen-hour class week. These hours can be exceeded if the teacher agrees. The college will increase the pay for each hour above the 16 hours. At this time the average rate of pay is about 3,000 RMB, more or less, for the basic 16 hour week in larger cities. Salaries depend on location and the budget of the college, so it could be considerably less. Monthly salaries do change according to the Provincial FAO policies from one year to the next. The salary you will receive is sufficient to live on for each month's expenses where you are working, but will not allow for many extras.

Welcome to China!

Arriving in China for the first time is a wonderful experience. Authorities from the college, university, or middle school where you have contracted will be very kind and gracious, doing everything they can to help you settle in and adjust. Your school's Foreign Affairs Office will arrange your transportation from the airport to your new living quarters by sending a member to greet you. This FAO member will be responsible for attending to your personal needs while you are working there. When you arrive in China, you will be working under three administrative authorities on campus. You will find them all very congenial:

First, the above mentioned Foreign Affairs Office will handle all of the work of securing your green card and the Foreign Experts card. Once you receive the green card, you no longer have to carry your passport. The green card contains your passport number. Be sure to locate that passport number on your green card, because sometimes bank clerks and other Chinese employees are not familiar with the green card. You use your green card as your visa document when you travel, and you'll need it for ID and checking into hotels and flying out of airports. You should carry this with you any time you go off campus or travel extensively inside China. Keep your passport in a safe place at home. Sometimes the director of the FAO is called a *Waibon* (Chinese meaning, *foreign office*), in case you hear that term. You usually receive your monthly pay through the Foreign Affairs Office.

Secondly, The Foreign Language Department – FLD – or the English Majors Department – EMD – You will consult the office under which you work regarding class schedule, textbooks, your syllabus (if required), and submission of all student grade records at the end of each semester.

And finally, the college Communist Party Secretary who represents the State authority on campus – This school official will probably arrange your welcome when you arrive on campus. Many colleges have a special dinner in honor of their foreign teacher(s) soon after they arrive, and this official is responsible for that courtesy.

In my several years of living and teaching in China, I have found the people supervising in these capacities to be extremely accommodating and helpful. Without exception, they have been very pleasant people and very easy to work with. In fact, many of them have become my personal friends, and I have stayed in contact with them after we parted from the same campus. On a couple of occasions, I have been invited back to lecture or take part in their summer programs.

Preparing to Teach

Most schools and colleges pretty well leave what and how you teach and grade the students up to the teacher. You will want to discuss this with your school after you arrive and before you begin your classes. The only exception is if you are coming to teach at a special professional college such as a medical institution. There is also a popular 2 X 2 foreign program allowing students to take two years of college with English in China, and then if they pass their level six International English Language Testing System – IELTS – exam, they enter a college abroad for some years. This is a special program that has several periods of special study preparing the students for the level six English exam. However, there won't be a lot of pressure on you, the foreign teacher, other than to fulfill general requirements such as submitting a syllabus – which I treat in a separate chapter – handing over final grades to the dean of your department at the end of each semester, and being present and on time for your classes. Other than that, methods, class procedures, class events, and when to hold exams are pretty well left up to the foreign teacher. There is no attempt to control or monitor the foreign work. For this reason and with this freedom, we should do our best to perform well as foreign teachers. I am speaking here for only Oral English courses. Other courses have much more demanding requirements, especially for the subjects carried by the Chinese teachers in the middle schools.

When you greet your first classroom of smiling Chinese faces full of enthusiasm and respect for their teacher, you will feel a great relief and surely fall in love with your kids!

Chapter Two
Understanding Your Students

The Chinese Temperament

When I made my first draft of this manual, it included a lengthy treatment of this subject. Most of the material was based upon my own experiences with the Chinese people that I have encountered in my work and social life, but I decided when I made the first edit not to try too stridently to convince my readers of the good traits of the Chinese people. You will quickly learn that through your own experience after a short time in China. The best advice I can give you here is to be friendly and smile a lot, and you'll be received as a native son or daughter wherever you go.

The word *friend* is an important word to the Chinese, and you will quickly make many friends. They honor friendship in a deeply sincere way. They never want to receive anything in return for any help or favors they bestow upon you. They are the most giving and helpful-natured people I have met in all of my travels over the world. The best way to give them something is in private, and sometimes after a brief but friendly wrestling match, assuring them it is a *secret,* and that it is our Western *culture* to do so. I have tried to give taxi drivers a little extra for waiting for me when I make a stop and then go on to another destination. This saves me having to pay an extra cab fare. Just a few days before writing these lines, I did this for a taxi driver who made several "waits" for me on a rainy day. He argued and refused the money saying it was "against the rules." Only after

I walked away and left the money on my seat did he reluctantly give up. It's very refreshing to me to live among people like this after traveling the world and having everyone from taxi drivers to border police try to extort money from you as the only means of getting past them. The graciousness of the Chinese people is especially appreciated when you consider that historically the Chinese have been oppressed and exploited by Western foreigners for centuries. In spite of that fact, they are extremely kind to foreigners to this day.

You will find the great majority of Chinese people to be cheerful, good natured, and polite. Many times Chinese ladies have offered me their seats on a crowded bus. They are patriotic, non-confrontational, even-tempered, and very caring toward others. You have heard of the proverbial man who always "makes a mountain out of a molehill"? Well, the Chinese person tends to make a molehill out of a mountain when it comes to faulting others for their misdeeds.

I must tell you a story to illustrate this typical attitude of the Chinese. One summer while teaching in Chongqing, I went with two other teachers to have lunch. We went to a nearby restaurant, and we all ordered beefsteak on rice. The meat was so tough, it was unfit to eat! I looked over at the two delicate little Chinese ladies, and they were laboring hard to chew the meat.

I said, "This beef is terrible! It's not fit to eat!" I was sure they would agree instantly with me.

But little Heidi said very seriously, "Mr. Bill, I think our knives are dull."

I said no more and went on chewing.

Understanding the Nature of the Chinese Student

Many Chinese students, especially in inland China campuses, come from a sheltered home life in the countryside. Some are extremely shy. Western teachers must understand that Chinese people are very conscious of saving face and can be hurt by being shamed or having anything happen that causes them embarrassment. This is extremely important for foreign English teachers to consider. One of the very sensitive characteristics of the Chinese is that they do not like to be denounced or put down when they make a mistake, but they are very quick to apologize when they have committed a wrong. I have had Chinese students apologize in tears after a class session for something I did not even consider a transgression. With that wonderful apologetic attitude we can afford to avoid open reproof. After a long acquaintance, reproof is well taken. Please don't think I am saying the Chinese student is perfect. I am describing the majority of the Chinese people. You may encounter the other kind of person, but rarely. My recommendation is to handle passive errors delicately, and aggressive errors should be handled privately and away from others when possible. Discipline may be sometimes necessary but only administered with utmost care and when guilt is apparent to all.

In sum, you'll never have better students than Chinese young people. Their motivation is far above average, and they are usually well focused in class compared to Western students. These qualities make teaching in China a pleasure for the foreign teacher who may have encountered less diligent student mentalities found in some Western cultures. As an international lecturer who has taught both adult and young adult students in more than twenty cultures, I can say that Chinese students are some of the most attentive of all students with whom I have worked.

The Chinese Spirit in the Classroom

It's a great boost to learning and very necessary when the teacher can have each student sound off in the classroom for oral exercises, drills, and pronunciation workouts. However, here again, it's best to wait until after the students have become acquainted for at least a month into the semester. Avoid using open student response with a new class at the beginning of a term, especially a freshman class. Freshmen are strangers and slightly intimidated by the new college environment. Many students are shy and come from backgrounds that honor this quality. The Chinese shyness is a precious social virtue and is considered by this teacher as one of the finer qualities of character. Sad to say, this quality is being lost in the recent generation. Some foreign teachers are not accustomed to such shyness. You can damage your relationship with the students and impede your purposes to communicate and teach well if this virtue is not respected.

Here are some recommendations that will help you to accommodate the shy nature of the Chinese student:

1. Give any freshman class at least five to six weeks to become acquainted with each other and with you before making open corrections in class.

2. Chinese people love to laugh and live relaxed lives. In the classroom do a little pantomiming or use humor. It will ease your students' tension. A laugh relaxes the atmosphere better than almost anything. Relaxed stu-

dents who are comfortable and not being made uncomfortable will learn faster and perform better.

3. After you see the students are more relaxed in their interrelationship with the class, then you may start having them perform openly. Even the shyest student can participate in class, but remember that shy students should be handled carefully. For example, while practicing a very difficult word to pronounce, if you make fun of the student or use him or her as a bad example of pronunciation you will set yourself back and make that student extremely hesitant to perform again openly.

4. One of the best methods of relaxing the shy student is to explain to the class why mistakes are important and fun in Oral English class. I always am careful to get across the following messages:

First, Oral English is a class that teaches the spoken language of English and so speaking is an important part of learning in this particular class.

Secondly, making mistakes in spoken English is important to the whole class! "Remember, when you mispronounce a word that half of the class is saying it the same way you are saying it." When a student mispronounces a word and lets me correct that mispronunciation, it is not only a help to that particular student, but also many of the other students who have the same problem.

Thirdly, I explain to the students that one way we learn many good lessons is through our mistakes and then having those mistakes corrected, and that mistakes are common in the learning process.

Mispronunciation can sound funny and make others laugh. I tell the story of the American visiting Peru who jumped onto a trolley car full of people. When the trolley suddenly lurched forward, he lost his grip on the overhead strap and fell onto the lap of a big lady. He was learning Spanish at the time and quickly started to search his mind for what he should say in Spanish as he sat there on her lap.

He turned and said to the lady in his best Spanish, "Permit me."

In Spanish, "permit me" is very close to the sound of "pardon me." He meant to apologize, but because his Spanish was so poor, he asked her for permission to sit on her lap!

There are many funny sounds and meaning changes involved in pronunciation errors, so I encourage my students to enjoy these humorous times as a community. Together we learn and laugh our way along the journey toward better English. I always encourage them to remember that now they may be laughing at me, but the next time I may be laughing at them! This explanation makes the students more comfortable with their mistakes, and some of our best times together are when we are all struggling with a difficult sound and laugh with each other in a drill. As a result of such a climate of good will and humor, I have not had one student ever embarrassed when he or she dropped a funny sound that caused others to laugh. Chinese students are very open to learning, and they listen well. Students, especially after they are acquainted with each other, accept this explanation very well and because they do like to laugh, they seem to welcome the explanation.

Still, each student's individual personality must be taken into account as I lead them down the path of "learning while we laugh." Once I had an extremely shy girl in class who would blush when I would ask her to say anything and would reply in almost a whisper.

She would then look up at me with a shy smile. I kept commending her until I saw she was ready to be corrected – carefully corrected. She eventually learned to make mistakes with the rest of us and enjoy it. There are always those students who enjoy making the others laugh at them, but I have never had a Chinese student take advantage of this and act a clown to get a laugh. The errors are always made in a sincere effort to give a correct pronunciation. I must emphasize that those students who are particularly shy must be handled like a piece of delicate crystal to avoid causing irreparable damage.

I recommend that you slowly lead them into what I call a *state of freedom of speech* before their classmates. I always let the shy members of the class guide me as to how and when to get the class rolling in full gear for open oral response. Within five to six weeks you will have everyone smiling and relaxed. After six weeks we have some hilarious times together, and we are learning while we laugh over our mistakes. If you are careful to lead the class into the habit of accepting mistakes as a part of learning, that's a great achievement for you and the class. You will deserve the badge of respect they will give you.

In terms of geographical demographics, there are two kinds of students in China's colleges and middle schools: those from the city and those from the countryside. The students from the countryside are probably more reserved than the city students and maybe even a little intimidated by their new surroundings away from home. If you're teaching in or around the large coastal cities like Guangzhou, Hong Kong, or Shanghai, you will find a more modern mind-set that compares better with the Western mentality. These young people come from the more developed areas of China and, in plain language, they are more materialistic and will think and act differently than the students from the countryside. Young people from the countryside have different values than young people from the city environment whose parents may be business people and more affluent.

Students attending middle school are there because it's required of them. The college setting is an altogether different atmosphere. The college student knows his college career is very important to his future. These students usually understand the importance of education and know that they must study hard to better their futures and make their parents proud of them. In many cases, students are only able to be in college because their parents have struggled, working long, hard hours in miserable cold and blazing sun and doing without in order to scrape up the money to get their children through college. Many of those parents want a better life for their children than they had, and they believe education will get them that better life. Many Chinese students have come to college through sacrifice, having a special appreciation for the opportunity of an education.

I urge my freshmen classes not to exchange the values they learned from their parents and their grandparents for the loose life and the free spirit they may see in certain students in the upper classes. I teach them that they should imitate those who love them and not the Michael Jacksons and the Back Street Boys who don't give a hoot for their wellbeing or their feelings. (There is a human tendency to aspire to be like popular entertainment celebrities!) The worse thing a teacher can do to precious young men or young ladies is to break that bond of credibility between them and their parents. I give strong lectures on "freedom" and decisions based on physiological urges as opposed to intelligent decisions based on conscience and moral sensitivity, as well as the difference between character and personality. I speak to my students about the pain of love, the vicarious nature of love that time heals, about changes in life, and other quality life issues that will guide them through the tough spots in their unknown future. That is all a part of being a good teacher.

A Word to the Wise for Male Teachers

Let me repeat an important principle for teachers: Sometimes to be better teachers we must be open to learning from our students. This also applies to our behavior as teachers of students of both sexes. If you want to have a good reputation among your students and your colleagues, then you must be sensitive to their cultural and ethical standards as it pertains to physical proximity between those of the opposite sex. This is particularly true of Western men who come here to teach and who may have the bad habit of touching the ladies.

Eastern and Western cultures are very different in this respect, and this difference should be carefully observed when you arrive in China. I have lived in more than fifty different cultures on five continents over the past forty-five years. I learned a little secret many years ago that will help keep you out of trouble when you're trying to adjust and be acceptable to your host culture. When I am not familiar with cultural standards while traveling, I watch the people I am among. In your observation, you will notice that touching between the sexes is not the practice of the great majority of students.

The vast majority of the physical contact between students, especially in the inland campuses, is between girls with girls and boys with boys, but hardly ever between boys and girls. You may see more contact between boys and girls in the more westernized coastal cities of China, because the coastal cities have been more exposed to the influences of the encroaching Western culture. You should take notice of the cultural behavior around you and then behave likewise. Don't fall prey to the mistake of believing that your Western culture that tolerates looseness of physical contact between the sexes is superior to the Eastern (Chinese) cultural habits, and that you're "going to liberate your students from their restrictive cultural traditions." That attitude will instantly alienate you from some very nice Chinese people. You are in China, and when you are here you would be wise to follow the prevailing cultural standards. These standards are highly civilized, arguably more so than in the Western countries. Western men come here to teach, not touch. Be careful.

Of course, it is a good practice to conclude that any man in any culture, Eastern or Western, who is discreet and respectful toward ladies, keeps his hands to himself. That is considered gentlemanly behavior in most parts of the globe. Let those of us who come from the West respect this cultural value and, again, *When in Rome, do as the Romans do.* These precious little Chinese girls will tell you they love you, and that you are handsome. The Chinese are extremely complimentary, but it has no sensual connotation whatsoever, and you should not take it as such. One girl sent me an e-mail with the subject heading: *I will love you forever.* She meant nothing by it. In fact, she was a shy little thing from the countryside. Flower language is common among the Chinese, as you will learn after being here a short time. Keep your distance physically, but tell your classes that you love them. They like to hear that very much!

While we are on the subject of crossing cultures, I would add one more bit of advice about telling jokes. Out of about twenty attempts to tell a joke in class that may add a good emphasis to our discussion I can only remember two I told that my students caught the punch line. Trying to tell a joke across cultures will flop about 80% of the time! That's not a good percentage. Your students will just sit and look at you with a dense look on their faces. You get into really deep trouble when you then try to explain the joke and why it's funny. I tried to tell my students the "Knock, Knock" routine. It was a catastrophe. If I saw just one student who thought it was funny and caught on, I quickly asked him to stand and explain it in Chinese. I'll warn you, that strategy also usually ends in disaster. I have learned to stay away from jokes unless I try them first in a circle of my Chinese friends on a social occasion outside the classroom. If they go over well in a private attempt, then I may tell them in the classroom when they will add to the discussion at hand. Of course, off color jokes are always out of place with students.

Positive Teacher, Positive Atmosphere

Many times, teachers do not know what some students are going through when they are sitting in the classroom. I have had students going through very traumatic times. A radiant personality is like the sun; it makes everybody feel so much better, and sometimes forget his or her troubles. The fact is that as teachers we have a lot to do with creating a good learning atmosphere. If students are coming into a classroom where they know they will be met with a smile and a kind word, they will look forward to those classes, but if you come into class at the last minute saying nothing, facing your class as if it was a drudgery to do so, they will sense your attitude, and this will affect their interest in class. A teacher that replaced me at one college turned out to be a grump. The students called me and sent e-mails about his angry words in class, sometimes crying. They were losing their former interest in the class. Young people simply learn more easily when they are enjoying a pleasant atmosphere. The teacher sets the tone for the class, creating an impression that learning is a pleasure. I can make my classes a delight or drudgery. It is the teacher's personality and pleasant loving attitude that charge students with the desire to learn.

When the students start filing in, you should be there, waiting with a smile, a comment, a greeting, with concern if they are limping or have a cold. A good teacher can do two things well: He or she can create the positive atmosphere that makes learning a wonderful experience, and then in that atmosphere impart speech skills they could not have learned in a dismal classroom with a grumpy, dry instructor. You may have the knowledge that can help them, but why not make that learning experience unforgettable by creating a bond of love between yourself and the student?

Chapter Three
The Central Goal of the Oral English Program

Why Foreign Teachers of Oral English?

The Bureau of Education in Beijing has brought you here to compliment what the Chinese English teachers are teaching in their English classes. You have something to offer the Chinese student that the Chinese teacher cannot give them: the pure sound of native English. In Oral English, the student becomes familiar with the sounds of native English pronunciation.

Students come to college with a very strong sense of anticipation about learning English under a foreign teacher. In fact, they dream of taking such a course, because in most middle schools they don't have foreign teachers. I decided to take a survey to learn what particular accomplishment my students expected to achieve in their Oral English class. In those surveys, I heard the same thing worded in one way or another from almost every student: They wanted to speak and learn better English *with* the foreign teacher. If that sounds a little simplistic (because it is naturally assumed), this simple goal of achieving a dialogue is nevertheless sometimes not accomplished, leaving the student and the teacher with an empty feeling of not having fulfilled a basic need.

It is easy to ascertain one's own goals for and the expectations of the students, but it is sometimes not so easy to actually achieve those aims. Throughout this book, we will discuss specific methods for fulfilling both our goals and the goals of our students.

Of course, we want to speak English in Oral English classes, but the big question remains, how do we *teach* spoken English? Let me now tell you it is much more than reading or telling stories. The answer is not to be found in videos or workbooks. I have used them all. The student of Oral English must do more than merely listen to English; he or she must hear it and speak it with an English-speaking person who can articulate clearly the spoken word. Foreign teachers of English must concentrate on their own clear and correct pronunciation to impart the language to their students. If you are not in the habit of enunciating clearly and speaking slowly, you must quickly get into the habit. Your pronunciation is your chief asset here in China.

Often I find that some foreign teachers misunderstand or fail to focus upon the central mission of the foreign teacher of English. We may have a vague idea of our job description, but nonetheless we lose track of the goal of improving our students' English pronunciation and meander our way into other things in our classes, such as speech or grammar.

A little grammar in Oral English is sometimes necessary. At the beginning of the term, with any new group of students, I always run through some basics such as consonants and vowels, phonics and syllables to help them sound out new words, and then I may have a ten question test on that lesson to help get the concepts lodged in their minds. I also refer to phonics sounds all through my term with my classes. By the end of the year, they can answer anything about sounds at the snap of a finger! However, once I establish these few basics as groundwork to help them with our real task, I quickly get back to what we do best as foreign teachers: teaching spoken English.

I have had foreign teachers tell me of discussions they have had in class on grammar that had become a big item, taking up a lot of class time, but English grammar can best be taught by the Chinese teacher. As Oral English teachers, we can get bogged down in grammar when the Chinese teacher is covering this subject very well. When we do this, we are failing our students and our call to China. All of our teaching methods are to further the end of achieving well pronounced English, whatever the size of the students' vocabulary or their fluency in English. Your students are getting grammar, composition, writing, and speech in other classes by proficient Chinese teachers. As a spoken English teacher I want to give these students what the Chinese teacher cannot offer them in their Chinese classes, and that is the English pronunciation of a native English-speaking person.

The more my students can speak with me, the better. The more exposure they have to my English speech and pronunciation, the better. That is the main reason behind the national education department providing Oral English classes, especially to English majors in Chinese colleges.

Remember, "If the English language is the mountain we seek to conquer, vocabulary is the route to the summit, but pronunciation *is* the summit." Many teachers believe that good pronunciation with a small vocabulary is better than poor pronunciation with a big vocabulary. I have had several outstanding students with large vocabularies who could not be understood because their pronunciation was so poor. I like to find such students and work with them on their pronunciation with a little special coaching. If I can give their vocabulary good pronunciation, I will have developed excellent two-way comprehenders. Vocabulary gives students the ability to understand you, but pronunciation assures that your students will be understood by the English-speaking person.

True English speech comprehension is made possible through the skill of good pronunciation. Chinese English teachers with whom I work are so accomplished in their English because of their ability to pronounce the language so correctly. When I talk to some of my Chinese colleagues, I forget I am speaking with Chinese people because their pronunciation is so good! That is the highest achievement in learning the English language – getting pronunciation up to the level of one's vocabulary.

Achieving pronunciation skills in your students is the ultimate evidence of the teaching skill of the Oral English teacher. Every one of the teaching methods we choose to use should contribute something to pronunciation. The teaching methods outlined in this manual all primarily target pronunciation, although they have lots of secondary instructional merit as well. I lectured regional middle school teachers during a teachers' conference one year and placed all of my teaching emphasis on pronunciation. The reason? Most of my students who come to me in college have been taught incorrect pronunciation. Let's take, for example, the word *usually*. Not one Chinese teacher out of 40 pronounced this word correctly! This means they have been sending every one of their students from their classroom out into the world pronouncing that word, and many others, incorrectly. I was very eager to hold lectures with these teachers because by helping them, I would be helping literally hundreds and thousands of students who would pass through their classrooms in upcoming years!

Remember, the educational department of the government of China has created the position of the foreign expert of English as integral to the proper education of the Chinese student in the English language. They don't need foreign teachers to teach anything but proper pronunciation. The Chinese teachers themselves can teach everything **but** correct English pronunciation. They don't need teachers of French or Japanese or German to teach how to read, write, and understand the grammar of the foreign language. They have extremely competent Chinese teachers and textbooks that do that. But, they do not have the ability to speak the language accent free in its native form. That is why we are in China. We take the Chinese students they have been teaching for up to seven or eight years and teach them to pronounce the English language that has been so aptly taught them by their Chinese teachers. We must concentrate on our objective and always remember that we are here to give to the Chinese students of English the one thing their Chinese teachers cannot give them – native English pronunciation.

Students feel uneasy when they are not making progress. They may even come to the conclusion that the teacher's methods are inadequate. Very often, this is the case. However, even though they feel this inadequacy, they are not sure what should be done to correct it. They just know they are not getting what they feel they need, what they expected to get from their class. So, in desperation, they may come up with ideas they hope will satisfy their desire to improve their English skills. Remember, they are very motivated to achieve their educational goals! They usually get such ideas from discussions they hold among themselves in the dorm and the dining hall. Students evaluate their classes and their teachers as well as the college they are attending. They are searching for an answer to their feeling that they are not quite getting what they want to be getting through their Oral English course. Many times the most vocal student on this score is one who is not terribly studious. All teachers have run into this type of student, the kind of student who can describe his feelings of inadequacy but has no logical plan to solve his problems.

I had such a boy in one of my classes, an LC student who was always ready with advice. This student came to me in class one day and suggested that the class members each be allowed to make a ten-minute speech at the beginning of every class. He insisted they needed to make speeches to improve their English. I always respectfully consider what any student says who seeks the good of the class. I asked him how many students said they wanted to do this.

He smiled broadly and said, "Two or three."

So, I agreed to run it past all of the students and see what they had to say. When I did, there was no enthusiasm at all for the idea (probably because they were giving speeches in other English classes), but several more, about six in all, raised their hands to give a speech. I limited the speeches to five minutes and passed a paper through the class and asked those to sign who wanted to give a speech. Six students out of thirty-two signed the paper.

I asked the boy to be the first, seeing as it was his idea. He gladly accepted and came to the next class prepared to give a "speech." He told a joke in less than two minutes – and it wasn't even funny! There I stood with my clipboard and pen in hand ready to evaluate his "speech" and list some words for correction and discussion.

When he finished telling his joke, he looked over to me and smiled with that broad smile again and said, "That's all, thank you," and returned to his desk.

You might say it was a bad experience, but for many reasons, that "bad" experience turned out to be a good experience in disguise. I learned some big lessons about teaching Oral English from the speeches that were given. I learned a lot about my students' actual comprehension skills. I learned whether they were even capable of being extemporaneous. I learned that many of them lean totally on memorization and reading to speak intelligible English in class. I learned they had very little ability to be extemporaneous or conversant.

With that fact established, I started placing a heavy emphasis on being original, creative, and extemporaneous. I reviewed phonics and word structure, vowels and consonants, syllables and sounding out the words, so they could read words they had never seen before. Then I buckled down on pronunciation and familiarization with the language. I listed all new words we found in class, copied the list in my class diary, and then wrote them on the board for review in the next class. I removed all memorization and reading of speeches from my oral classes! The only exception was when they were reading *with me*. I turned up the heat on giving students lots of opportunity to speak English through Read Along, Talk Along, Follow Along, and discussions. The students were *all* able to speak *with* me in this way. The students' response was electric. Participation was up and a new sense of fulfillment was charging the classroom atmosphere. They were speaking and reading English *with* a native English-speaking person. It was fulfilling to them and their teacher.

When they had given those ill-fated speeches, I noticed that they memorized and used words in their speeches of which they did not even know the meaning! I wrote down words they used in their speeches and asked them the meaning of the words when they were finished, and they couldn't answer. I had instructed them not to memorize, but they did anyway because they had to. If they didn't memorize what they were going to say, they couldn't give a speech. Several students had memorized the same articles and gave them word for word in different classes. On the other side of the coin, I also discovered the students in my class who could speak very well and even casually without memorization.

By allowing those speeches I discovered what my tasks were in teaching Oral English. Memorization and speeches serve a purpose in learning a language, but in spoken English we want the students to become conversant and skilled in English. To accomplish this they must learn to handle the language independent of memorization and become completely self competent.

I also discovered they were not following instructions sometimes because they were not comprehending me. I had instructed them clearly, with the help of my student tutors, that their speeches were not to be memorized or written. Only a few of my best students complied with the speech rules while the others – the great majority – of students relied on memorization.

To be better teachers, we sometimes have to learn a few things from our students. It may sound over-simplified, but *to speak English, they must speak English.* The methods I provide in the following chapters will allow the students to speak the language with a native speaker – that's you. To speak English with you is what they want to do, and it is what they need to do. They should be oral in their oral classes, and it is important to always keep this in mind. Discussion with the teacher is one of their favorite exercises. This is one of the things I learned when I took a student poll on teaching methods. I asked many classes what they felt was the most beneficial method of learning English for them: reading along with me, hearing me talk in lectures (learning articulation), open discussions, word studies, or whatever. In this manual are the top methods that both my students and I have found to be the most effective and the explanations why they are successful.

Chapter Four
Basic Class Structures

My habit is to be in my classroom twenty to thirty minutes before class is to begin, when that is possible. I like to be in my classroom with the lights and fans on and everything alive and ready when the students start arriving. It's good for student morale to create a positive class atmosphere right from the beginning. When the classroom is alive and warm, and the teacher is there, smiling to greet them as they file in for class, it sets a good tone. If the class is in a room being used by another class before me, then I like to be right there so I am one of the first to enter the class.

Here are some other organizational details that will help to create a solid structure for learning:

English Names

It's easier for the teacher to relate to the students personally if each student has a name card displaying the student's English name. Even if you have a good knowledge of Chinese, it creates an English language atmosphere if we are calling each other by English names. Anything you can do to create thinking in English is beneficial. Students are usually eager to have an English name. Students who are not in my classes come to me frequently and want me to give them English names. I am always ready with a few good names in mind when I'm among students on occasions such as English Corner (See Chapter Twelve.) or when I am invited to a student activity. Most students have an English name by the time they reach college, but some do not. One of the first things you will want to do in your very first meeting with a class is to make sure that each student has an English name and that you are well on your way toward remembering those names.

Name cards will help. A simple piece of paper, about 1/4 of a standard sheet of stationery paper, can be folded lengthwise and then set up on the desk with the fold upward. This way the name can be printed clearly with a dark marker, easy for the teacher to see as he walks through the class. You can have them write their English name on one side and their Chinese name in Pinyin on the other if you want to become familiar with their Chinese names.

Seating Charts

Establishing a seating chart can be a very important way to effectively work with your lower comprehending students in class. As soon as all students get their English names, then I assign seats. Once seats are assigned, the students are asked to keep those seats and not move without permission from the teacher. I ask them not to change seats because I have my monitors check any absences in their classes. When each student stays in their assigned seat, we can easily see who is absent and who is present. This allows my monitors or me to know immediately who is absent as each class starts. In a class of 32 students, I make a chart with 32 blocks and write the English and the Chinese name in the seating block. It also helps me locate my students by name if I am at my desk. You can also record oral exam scores in the seating boxes or place minus signs in the seating blocks for class performance demerits.

Students usually buddy-up in pairs and often stay chums through their college days. Naturally, they like to sit together in class. In my seating, however, I cannot always take these friendships into consideration if I want to do my best job of teaching. I do leave friends together when I possibly can, but I know that they have other opportunities to be together. In my class I want them to excel in spoken English – that's all. To help them I must seat them in such a way that the high comprehenders, or HC's, are scattered throughout the class to help those with the lower comprehension. Here is just another instance in which you will see the wonderful attitude Chinese students tend to show when their personal preferences have to be set aside for the academic good of the class. They all comply happily and leave their friends after I give an explanation. You will never hear a whimper come from Chinese students so long as they understand your reasons.

It is my opinion that seating should be based upon the Entrance Comprehension Level Score, or ECLS. The low comprehenders, or LC's, are my great concern, and I want to give them special attention. This is why I refer to my LC's as *special* students. I determine my class seating arrangement as soon as I administer the ECLS. I carefully seat the high comprehenders among low comprehenders. I usually seat my lowest comprehenders in my front rows. This is especially good in a larger classroom where you may at least have eight seats across. The front row of special students is always stationary until I move them. Then each month, I have the other rows rotate. The back row moves up to the second row's place while the second and each remaining row move back one space.

First, I total the scores of the ECLS. I divide the number of students into that total, and that gives me the average comprehension of that class. I consider the students below that average score as my low comprehenders. Students with a score above that average are my high comprehenders. In every class you will have a few very low comprehenders and a few very high comprehenders.

Class Rosters

There are two basic methods our college English departments use in assembling their class rosters. The first is to arrange classes in the order of the student's comprehension level. Upon entering the freshman year and every year thereafter, individual students are given the ECLS to determine their comprehension. A student roster list is prepared with the HC's at the top of the list and the LC's at the bottom of the list. This list is then divided into four classes starting with the top 32 students. This way you have students with approximately the same comprehension in each class. This method does allow the teacher to better zero in on one level of teaching and is considered the ideal by some teachers. Schools, colleges, or universities that adopt this method must necessarily give every entering freshman an ECLS, unless they are assigning classes based upon the student's grades in all subjects (which this teacher does not endorse). Proponents of this method argue that by lumping students of similar skill-levels together, you can be more effective in teaching and raising the student's skills. This method of class arrangement has its advantages. The main advantage is being able to teach those high comprehenders on their level and take them to higher levels of comprehension.

The second method used is to randomly assign students to classes with no consideration of their English comprehension. This also has its advantages. In this case the teacher has high comprehenders mixed in with low comprehenders and can use the more proficient students to help the lower achievers as we have mentioned in regard to class seating. High comprehenders can be seated in the class in such a way that they can assist the teacher in helping the LC's. Both of these methods have their advantages. However, as I mentioned, I do not believe in placing students based upon their overall grade point average. This method does not identify the LC students and doesn't give you the kind of information that you will need to devise your teaching strategy. A student with a low grade in physics may have a very high comprehension level, but because of his lack of competence in physics, he will not be placed in an HC English class but more probably will find himself placed in a lower class. Basing class rosters on overall grade points across the curriculum ends up creating classes with mixed levels of comprehension and does not achieve the aim of sorting students appropriately.

My preference is the random class arrangement. I have found that high achievers can really help the teacher and the LC's while at the same time benefiting from taking a role of increased responsibility in class and becoming an authority in English. Working closely with the teacher as an assistant is a great educational experience for the student tutor, but this method is not the best for some teachers who may choose not to integrate student helpers into the organization of the class. The important thing is that we are each effective in bringing our students' level of English language skills up.

I always make a list of all students in the order of their ECLS, ranking the high scores at the top and the lowest scores at the bottom. This is a reference list for me when I need to know a student's comprehension level at a glance. I also use it to help me to seat my special students in the front rows of the class.

The LC's need more of my attention. I do more one-on-one with them, giving them more special attention and stopping at their desks to work out their pronunciation and vocabulary problems. When they do something well, I commend them before the class to encourage them. I also want to push my higher comprehending students to even higher levels of success. I achieve this by giving the HC's an opportunity to serve as class secretaries and teacher's assistants. Class secretaries help me do in-room tasks such as looking up a new word or standing and giving its definition in Chinese if no one else volunteers. I will ask the HC's to help me with students who are struggling with a difficult pronunciation problem, or those having a hard time understanding what I am saying, or understanding a text we are reading. The HC's help me to provide more one-on-one assistance to my LC's. During discussions, I engage and call upon HC's because they enjoy discussion and benefit by it. These have to be exceptional comprehenders, and every class will usually have about three to six such students. Having my HC's assist me in class gives me more personal contact with these students and gives them more opportunity to dialogue with me. The HC's generally highly value the opportunity to speak privately with the teacher as it greatly sharpens their conversational English skills.

I would not be able to tailor my approach toward my students if the ECLS were not there to help me identify my students' skill levels from the outset. Without the ECLS, I might get a sense of skill level and individual need after several weeks or months. The ECLS allows me to know, from my second class forward, who needs extra assistance and who might benefit from extra responsibility in the classroom.

But let us return to seating. With the knowledge provided by the ECLS, I can now reseat the class so that the high and low comprehenders are mixed in such a way that the better students are spread evenly throughout the class nearer the special students who are in need of more help.

Then when I am doing, for example, a Read Along and there is a difficult passage, I stop and say to the students, *"Help each other!"*

They then are free to talk in Chinese and discuss what we are saying to the class. You may also ask one of your secretaries to just stand and explain in Chinese what has been read for all to hear. This helps struggling students. When I want the students to confer with each other, I make a motion with my elbows as if I'm nudging the person on either side of me. They soon learn by that motion that I want them to discuss this difficult sentence or subject amongst themselves in Chinese. This is the way I compensate for not having both languages. The Chinese teacher has a great teaching advantage by knowing both languages.

Another way to help those straggling behind in class is to encourage them to raise their hands if they have a question I may have raised in their minds while I was speaking. To encourage them, I simply explain that when they ask a question, others will most likely have the same question, and thus, when I answer their question they have helped the whole class find the answer. This explanation motivates them to ask questions. Participation can be developed in a class by reminding students of the benefits of their involvement. I continuously tell them why it's important to raise their hands.

It may be the practice of many foreign English teachers to avoid using any language but English in the oral classes. I myself once strongly adhered to that policy. Now, however, I try to be a little more flexible and tend to allow a bit of Chinese to be spoken for the sake of my LC students during brief discussions. I soon noticed that allowing Chinese did seem to help the LC's to find their bearings on occasion.

You will soon find that having your HC's spread evenly through the class seating is a tremendous help. The Chinese temperament is one that values helping and being kind to others, so giving attention to other students who need more help is a pleasure for the HC's and appreciated by the special students. Remember again that in a freshman class, we should wait until probably near mid-semester, after the students are well acquainted, to implement this program. In fact, I find it wise to gradually introduce my different teaching methods so that students can become accustomed to and comfortable with each.

Let's stop right here for a moment and remind our readers that this principle of high comprehending students helping those who are struggling is a teaching method that can be used in any class by any teacher whether you teach mathematics, biology, or a speech class. Not allowing students to help one another wastes a great deal of potential in the classroom. Struggling students can benefit from extra one-on-one attention, and advanced students can find their skills sharpened by consulting with the teacher and explaining difficult concepts and skills to other students.

Class Monitors and Secretaries

The Foreign Language Department usually appoints monitors for each class. Monitors are responsible for passing on all announcements to their classes regarding school activities. They are the go-betweens for the dean's office and the students. I also appoint at least two additional class secretaries to assist me in all kinds of duties from handing out and collecting papers to helping me keep my class records through the school year, including the making out of the term grades. I choose these secretaries after several weeks of observing class performance and based upon their ECLS. The class monitors check class attendance each day and lay a brief written report on my desk quietly without disturbing the class. Once or twice a year I take my monitors and secretaries out to lunch to discuss class activities and express my appreciation to them for their great assistance to me.

Student Tutors

Looking at my CLS sheet after several weeks into the term, I appoint students with proven high comprehension in the class to serve as tutors. I meet with these students in a special session and explain to them their duties. Being singled out for exceptional performance is encouraging to them, and they take their responsibility to help other students very seriously. Not only that, but in order to help others to the best of their ability, my HC's tend to apply themselves to a greater degree in class. As I said, Chinese people, and especially the young people, enjoy helping others.

Chapter Five

Documentation: A Source of Order in the Classroom

Grading Records

Each college setting has its own system of grading requirements. I have graded under two systems. The middle schools usually use the simpler method of grading based on 100 possible points, while many colleges will use a coefficient system that divides the grade into two or more separate grades, and then final scores can be determined by averaging the total scores. This process will be carefully laid out in an upcoming chapter.

You will have to have grade sheets completed and handed in to the Dean of the English Language Department at the end of each school semester. I design my own grade sheets and print them myself, and then have my class secretaries help me figure and fill them out. You may want to consult one of the Chinese teachers about how they submit their semester grades. In most American colleges, teachers have their own office and usually a capable student or even a professional secretary. You will not have those luxuries here in China, so I select a few of my best students to help me with all the recording of grades. I check out their work, and then collate the class records and staple them together with cover sheets and hand them in. They are then ready to be presented to the office of the Dean of the English Department. They should be submitted on the date specified by the dean's office. Be sure to make an extra copy or two for safekeeping. One year the office lost my records, and if I had not kept two extra copies, we would have been up the creek without a paddle!

Provide a nice cover sheet for each class record, with five elements of information on that cover:

a.) The title – Semester Grade Sheet – at the very top

b.) The name of the class in big letters

c.) The name of the teacher of the class

d.) The date period the records cover

e.) The name of the college or university and the department

See example below.

Figure 5.1

Grade Sheets for Second Semester

February 3, 2006 through July 7, 2006

Class III Oral English

Mr. Bill

English Department

ULI

Zhengzhou, Henan

Including a cover sheet on grade records submitted to the dean's office makes the record keeping in the office much easier.

Class Record Books

Your personal class record books will help you immensely as long as you teach. I will explain my system as an example and perhaps a starting place, but of course you will eventually develop your own system. It is important that you have an accurate and well-organized record of your classes. My class record books consist of the following items:

Class Seating Chart

As mentioned previously I always print out a class seating chart. The chart consists of a header with the class name and the school name at the top. My name is also included in the event the chart is lost on campus. In a simple boxed format, I have the Chinese and the English name of every student written in each box according to his or her seat assignment. Also in this box I write the ECLS and record any special behavior of the student, good or bad, that would affect his grade. I usually place initials such as an "A" in the box containing that student's name, then in the margin of the chart I write that initial (letter) and the meaning of it. Example: "A: Absent 3 classes" in small letters. If necessary, you can also make a small minus mark (-) meaning he slept or broke a class rule. If he spat on the floor, you may want to make 5 minus marks! (That's serious!) My seating chart is well marked with notes and scores by the end of each semester. It contains a concise but good record of the student body in that class.

Class Directory

Another thing that I have started recently and keep in my record book is the class directory. This has already proven to be a big help. I hand out a half sheet of paper and have students write their name, date, and class at the top. Then I ask them to answer a handful of simple questions:

1. English name?

2. Chinese name in Pinyin?

3. Hometown?

4. Home phone?

5. Dorm phone?

6. E-mail address? (if they have one)

This information is then compiled into a class directory. The directory helps me to keep track of my students, learn their names, understand the geographical make-up of the class, and to contact a student should a need arise throughout the term. You'll be surprised how many times throughout the school year you may want to contact your students about class matters or for other important reasons.

Class Diary

The most important record I keep that helps me stay on course and maintain continuity of my teaching sessions is my class diary. I use a spiral notebook one half sheet in size. When you open it, it lays flat on your desk about the size of a full sheet of paper with one page on either side of the spiral as it lays open.

On the left hand page I make note of material I want to review with the class next period. When your class periods are sometimes days apart, this becomes a very important record! This way I don't have to go through the entire diary records to find the review. Also on the left hand page I make any special notes/comments that I want to remember and record class assignments. The page gives me information I need to find at a glance and lets me pick up where I left off in the previous class. It also links my class subject material and helps me keep the flow of my teaching from class to class. On this page I also keep notes on any class irregularities, student behavior (good and bad) and especially new inspirations for the next class period.

On the right hand page I keep a diary-like record of what subject material I covered in each class session. My entries on the right hand page in the diary appear something like the example shown below in *Figure 5.2*.

Figure 5.2

5-18-04 Read from reader p. 367; The three big bad words; Explained writing hard word phonetically on bb (blackboard); Business class: Defined the joint venture as being an agreement that is a mutual benefit to both parties. New words: "perks" China offers to foreign investors in tax breaks, etc., Dem. (Demonstrated) word "tease" by poking at the boys annoying them (fun!), laughing. Discussed the key to success in a private enterprise (service); Must offer a service to people. Gross and net profits, the cost of operation…

I usually have sufficient space for two class entries per page. When I finish class, I immediately enter the date of the next class and give the page on which we stopped reading in the readers so that I can pick up where we left off in the previous class. I am careful to make a note regarding what I will do in the next class carried over from the past class. For example, I made the above entry on May 18. I drop down several spaces and enter the date of that next class, 5-22-04, and enter the page number where we are reading and note the text in the reader as marked also. Now I am able to go right to the place we left off in the last class. However, in many class sessions we may not use the reader, so instead I enter what we were discussing when class ended. This will take two to three minutes to do at the end of each class. It's also wise to write the record for your first hour of class during the break between classes when possible.

As I mentioned, I usually come to class thirty minutes or more prior to class time unless getting from another class makes that impossible. The first thing I do is review the last two or three class sessions in my diary record book to be sure I pick up where I left off in the last class session.

Another invaluable use of the class diary record book is to be able to refer back to them from years past. Many times we teach some wonderfully inspired things on impulse rather than preparation. A record of those special inspirations can be recalled, polished, and used effectively again. The class diary books I have accumulated during my years in China become more valuable to me with each passing year.

The Syllabus

The syllabus is usually requested by the college you attend and amounts to your informing them of what your plans are for teaching and what materials you will be using. It could consist of just one sheet or many. The simpler you keep it, the easier it is for the college administration to file and refer to, but the syllabus should be accurate and informative. Following is an example of a syllabus in case your college requests it:

Figure 5.3

Oral English and Business English

Dr. Bill

For Term of August 2006 to July 2007

Classroom teaching materials to be used:

1. *Oral Workshop* Textbook No.2

2. Swiss novel: *Heidi*

3. Topical studies from the Oxford University Chinese/English study materials

4. Business Internet reports from SCMP, Beijing

5. Talk Along lectures on values in life.

6. Talk Along in the *Oral Workshop Discussion* readers.

7. Follow Along from *Chicken Soup for the Soul.*

8. Word Sheet pronunciation - *Secrets to Better English*

9. *Basic Enterprise Economics* chart

10. *Business English* manual provided by the college

All freshmen entering my classes this year will receive an Oral ECLS to determine:

(a) Each student's comprehension level

(b) The high and low comprehension range of the class

(c) The average comprehension of the class

(d) HC's to be used as student tutors and teacher's assistants in giving special assistance to low comprehension students.

Final grading will be based on the 30 and 70 coefficient system for class performance and exam performance. Three oral exams covering pronunciation, two-way comprehension, and continuity of speech will be given.

Sincerely submitted,

Dr. Bill

Foreign Teacher of

Oral and Business English

ULI

Zhengzhou, Henan

Chapter Six
Behavior and Decorum

Class Rules

I have a very good relationship with my students, and we have nice times together, both in the classroom and out, on campus and off campus, but I have classroom rules, fourteen of them, and I enforce them, and sometimes issue serious warnings to my students when they violate classroom conduct rules. Discipline is necessary to keep order in a classroom. In the Western educational environment discipline has gone to pot in many institutions, but rules are essential as a standard for everyone and to establish an order that is necessary to achieve peak efficiency. Most importantly, rules give the students the experience of working under conditions similar to those they will encounter as they enter the work place in the real world.

I explain to my students that in my classroom we are learning English to enter the work place, perhaps in a large corporation or a business of our own. Every one of my class rules has a parallel to the work place they will likely enter after college. I think of my classroom not only as a place to learn, but also as a place for training for the conditions many of them will meet in the secular work environment in the new enterprise corporate world. Many of the new business environments will have the proficiency of the parent organizations in the West, demanding high standards of behavior and appearance as well as skills and special abilities.

Each teacher usually forms his or her own classroom rules according to individual personality and philosophy on the matter. My classroom rules not only control the behavior of the student in class, but also prepare the student for his or her future. Here are my rules with explanations as to how they also apply to the work place.

Rule 1: *Carefully listen to instruction.*

Rule 2: *Carefully follow instructions.*

I stress these first two rules as the secret to communication. Communication is supremely important to all students when they get into the work place, but, alas, most people do not know what communication is, nor can they define it. It is much more than the exchange of ideas between two or more people. We do not communicate by speaking. Communication is listening! You may speak to others, but if they are not listening, there is no communication. If you are listening, it means someone is speaking, and that is when communication happens.

I always tell my students that when you are interpreting for someone, and they are explaining something, never, never, never say to them, *"I know, I know, I know!"*

From my own personal experience, this triple assertion actually means *"I don't know!"* I always get the wrong information when they say that.

Rule 3: *Be to class on time.*

This is a requirement of the workplace. If you're frequently late, you can lose your job over such negligence.

Rule 4: *Be nice to everyone.*

On the job and in real life, getting along with others can be the difference between success and misery. It's the first social rule of life. If you want to have friends, you must be friendly.

Rule 5: *Keep your hands and feet to yourself.*

When you're on the job, you must learn to do your own job well and not be poking your nose into other people's business (unless you're asked, and then be careful). If you have the urge to play, wait until you're three miles from your desk!

Rule 6: *Do not erase the blackboard unless asked to do so.*

Never touch another person's work unless you consult the person who put it there, especially if that person is a superior under whom you are working.

Rule 7: *Do not look on the teacher's desk.*

On the job, that is equivalent to the boss's desk. Learn now to not nose into papers and look at materials that you are not authorized or have not been asked to look at. Your boss will take a very dim view of anyone reading company directives that may contain restricted information.

Rule 8: *Raise your hand to speak.*

Learn the manners of conversation. Intelligent conversation is when all parties are able to express themselves in an orderly and calm manner. If we are all speaking at the same time, there is nothing intelligible accomplished, and order is lost. Unless we are having an open discussion, the polite thing is to be recognized by the person leading the meeting or conversation. Be acknowledged for permission to speak, and then speak. I practice this training during certain exercises and then lift it for most other activities where I want more action.

Rule 9: *Place all trash in the proper waste bins and receptacles.*

Do not trash the floors and desks, creating work for others because you are lazy or unclean. This rule is intended to deeply impress upon the student the problems of pollution and teach that we must not be a part of the pollution problem in China, but a part of the answer. I sometimes wad up a piece of paper and throw it on the floor to get the students' reaction.

I ask them, *"Is that right? "*

I get a resounding, *"Noooooooo!"*

Rule 10: *Do not spit on the floor unless you spit on your mother's floor at home!*

Dirty habits are not tolerated in the finer work places. If your office is clean when you get the job, then you know what is expected of you.

Rule 11: *Do not lay your head down and break eye contact with your teacher during class.*

Look your superiors in the eye when they speak to you. Your boss will appreciate your focus on him when he is speaking to you. Your attention reflects your true interest and disinterest.

Rule 12: *Do not talk in class unless you are assisting a classmate to understand the teacher.*

When the boss is talking, it's always important! You must not start a second conversation with your friend beside you when the boss is talking. This is a good way to lose his favor . . . and maybe your job.

Rule 13: *Do not abuse or deface classroom/company property or equipment.*

If you damage anything belonging to someone else, the proper thing to do is report it to your superiors. Graffiti, writing on desk surfaces, or abusing company equipment is frowned on in corporate environments. If you try to hide damage, it could cost you your job. Do the right thing: Report it and apologize.

Rule 14: *Dress appropriately. Do not wear shorts to class.*

In many prestigious corporate work places there will be a dress code that reflects a proper respect for yourself, your company, and those who work around you. One such company is IBM. Standards of modesty and proper behavior in the work place have been proven to yield higher production. Government dignitaries and respectful people wear classic clothing that reflects a serious-minded career mentality.

I have unwritten rules as well, such as *No books open from other classes during my class sessions.* In the work place they will be required to do only the work of the company they are working for and not bring other work of their own or for others to do on the time of the company that is paying them. Before the bell rings or between class sessions is the students' time, and they can then do other class work, but in the actual class sessions, I do not allow other materials from other classes to be open on the desk. I sometimes gather a book or two and then hand them back after the class session. In almost every case, and there aren't too many, the Chinese student will apologize and ask for forgiveness.

I also *do not allow mobile phones to be handled or used during class time.* If a student receives a call, I tolerate that. During break periods use of mobile phones is allowed in my class, but you may require they turn off their mobile phones during class.

Encouraging Participation

When I am doing Read Along or Talk Along exercises (more on these later), I move around, walking the classroom. As I walk, I do several things to encourage participation. First, I am listening to their pronunciation and voices as I move up and down the aisles past them. When I hear a student with incorrect pronunciation, I stop and move in closer to that student, repeating the word (with the class following my voice) and working with that individual student. Secondly, I stop on more difficult words or to pronounce new words that need to be defined and added to their vocabulary, especially words I know they can use and need in daily conversation. Thirdly, I watch for low participation efforts. I may see a student trying to read a textbook for another class behind his desk, which I do not allow, or a student preoccupied and looking out the window and not speaking along with me, or a student whose lips are barely moving. When I encounter a poor participator, I say nothing. I simply lock my eyes on him and move in closer and closer as I continue reading or speaking until he snaps out of it. I simply keep repeating one word, staring right at him, until he looks up at me and enters into full participation again.

500 Times!

If students behave defiantly in class, I have them write a sentence 500 times. The sentence, such as, "I should show respect to my teacher and my fellow students," is written on papers I provide. If they refuse, they go to the dean's office escorted by the class monitor. I use the "500 Times" discipline only in extreme cases of contempt or rebellion. I've had only one case in my years in China, but I can say it is very effective! It's more likely to have to be used in middle school classes than in the more serious and focused college classes.

The Pep Talk Lecture

If a student or students commit a gross violation of class rules, I will walk to the front of my classroom and give the whole class a strong five-minute pep talk explaining the purpose of our class and how much their parents are counting on them. I may talk about the students I have that are very high achievers because they put their soul into learning, or how important English is to them as the WTO generation of the new China of tomorrow. Every time I give a strong pep talk about class participation and the importance of having a good command of English, they always respond with vigorous renewed participation. The volume of voices triples! Like I say, they are good, responsive students who are concerned about their futures. They sometimes just have to be nudged a little to get them motivated and back on track.

Spring Fever

As mentioned above, when the weather begins to turn warm in the spring, we have a little spring fever chart I teach from that explains the effect of the barometer on the body and mind. It's also a time when we start having more outside activities that may cause the mind to wander. Sometimes brief information or explanation lectures can help to keep attention focused on their classes. I also feel that my corrective lectures help them in their other classes as well.

Chapter Seven
Read Along

Students like engaging in dialogue with the teacher, whether it's in class or out of class. This is an element of teaching that brings the student closer to the teacher. A friendly chat outside the class is especially good for students who are shy in the classroom. It's true that there are some students who are especially talkative and want to talk about nothing in particular sometimes, but providing equal time for each student is a good policy. One boy got my mobile phone number and called me in class to ask me if I was happy. I told him I was in class and couldn't talk now, but that I was very happy! He then sent seven messages to my mobile phone apologizing for calling me while I was still in class. You might say he defeated his purpose.

The approach I describe in this manual is concerned with achieving two-way comprehension of English in the student, not just one-way. Our objective is to bring the student to a conversant comprehension of English that allows him or her to carry on a dialogue with another English-speaking person. This is the ultimate objective for the foreign teacher and the student. The teaching methods we use should allow as much dialogue between the student and the foreign teacher as possible. To give the student this two-way conversational experience, there are three good methods that I will provide in this and the following chapters in the order of their effectiveness and *mental impact*.

Read Along

Read Along works like this: The teacher reads the text word-by-word or phrase-by-phrase and the students follow, *imitating* the teacher's pronunciation. This is a good method to take any class through a difficult text in any subject. When the text is tough, whether it's math, science, or Oral English, reading it with them and guiding them through helps the learning mind to comprehend.

Note to Oral English teachers: You can get any number of such readers with stories from the library or from the Internet and print them out if you're waiting for the manuals to come from the school office. Some schools will allow you to choose a *reader* if you have a preference. I recommend readers for Oral English. In my opinion they are preferable to workbooks because all of the other English classes use workbooks. In Oral English we are concentrating on the oral aspect of English and not composition or grammar as in the other classes. You need only a reader with short stories and preferably stories with a moral that will provoke discussion after you have read the story together. In Read Along, the class also benefits from having any new words spelled out before their eyes to underline and study after or before the discussion. Viewing the words as they are reading helps students with their spelling.

This is a pure form of responsive reading and gives the student the maximum number of mental impressions. He hears it (the sense of hearing) as he reads it (the sense of sight), then he speaks it (the sense of sound) as he reads it again. He hears the teacher reading in the sound of native English and then he hears himself imitating the native English sound. This is a very rich source of intellectual stimulation for the student, and it provides the best results for the process of learning a foreign language and achieving correct pronunciation because it makes five different mental impressions at once on the learner.

Responsive reading is one of the best methods we can use to expose the mind to the sound of a language. You read it twice and hear it twice. The first time, you hear it correctly from the English teacher; the second time, you hear it to correct yourself. The process goes something like this:

1. The teacher reads, and the students follow his/her reading of the text.

2. The student hears the teacher reading with native English pronunciation.

3. The student then reads the text again himself after the teacher in a responsive reading of what the teacher read.

4. When the student reads, he is speaking what he is reading.

5. When the student reads, he is hearing his pronunciation, and

6. Mentally comparing it with what he heard the teacher say.

During the Read Along process, the student is also talking *with* the foreign teacher, which helps to establish a beneficial, close working relationship. The process also helps to improve vocabulary. One easy way to make sure that the Read Along exercise is helping to improve vocabulary is to carefully select potentially unfamiliar words and take time to explain the meaning. This is also a good time to allow students to talk to one another in Chinese to discuss the meaning of the word. This helps the LC's to stay up with the rest of the class. We don't want anyone to be left behind.

To get across the meaning of new words, I first define the word to the class in simple terms that they will understand. Then I have students use their dictionaries to read the definition in both English and Chinese. Sometimes I have to enlist the aid of what I call "action teaching." I may have to use pantomime to illustrate the meaning of a new word that resists simple definition. For example, with the word *pester*, I may start poking at one of the students while I'm talking to the class explaining the meaning. Then after a while I ask him, "*Do you know what I'm doing? I'm pestering you!*" Everyone laughs and repeats the word.

During Read Along, I have them underline or make a list of the words with which they are not familiar. After finishing the story and the discussion that follows, we go over the list of words they want explained. Finally I have them form a sentence with the new word in it. I can do this in two ways:

1. I can ask them to respond verbally, voluntarily, or as I call on them.

2. I can give them each a small piece of paper and have them write a sentence with the new word. Then I read the papers to the class, never revealing names unless it is a very good answer, especially a good answer by an LC, recognition of which will be encouraging.

Always remember that when the class is slow to respond, it's usually because they did not understand you. In this case you must stop and ask one of the students who *did* understand you to stand and explain to the rest of the class in Chinese what you said. Then you might have them all talk together in English about it for a minute and then ask the question again. During this time, you can keep your eye on the LC's and be sure they are following along. You will see a different response once they all understand your question.

Once you have finished a Read Along, there are many secondary teaching methods that will reinforce and expand upon the learning experience: These techniques are explored throughout the manual, but let's present them here in a concise list so that you develop a clear sense of your options following the Read Along exercise:

1. Discussion: A good reader will end the stories in a predicament, so you can actually end the story with a number of conclusions through discussion. Any story worth using in class will be good discussion material. Students enjoy responding to and thinking through the stories, and this process exercises their comprehension skills and gives them a nice opportunity to practice their extemporaneous English conversation skills.

2. New words: As I mentioned, when reading a story from the readers, I instruct the students to underline any words with which they are not familiar. When we have finished the story and perhaps a discussion, I then ask for the words they underlined and write each new word on the board as we discuss it. For example, when I am reading a small novel such as *Heidi* to them, I have them underline words they do not understand, and then we go over the new words, and I illustrate what they mean. I also find the *Longman Contemporary Dictionary, New Version* to be very helpful in defining new words.

3. Board review: Don't let new words die with only one treatment. I sometimes copy those new words in my class diary and then write them on the board again in the next class session and go over them again for double impression. If I deem the words usable in their everyday use of English, I may review them several times and even give a mini exam – a 5-10 question quiz that goes on their grade – covering those words.

4. Sentence structuring: After you have treated it sufficiently, you can then ask them to construct sentences using the new word. They find this a little difficult, so you may have to call on them to get started. Call on your good students who participate well, first.

5. New words for the difficult words list: If we run into a word that is especially hard to pronounce, I write it in the margin of my class diary to remind myself to add it to my "difficult words list," what I call *The Word Sheet,* for future practice and review. I have included an example of this list in the upcoming chapter on pronunciation for your reference and perusal. This is a collection of approximately seventy words we have singled out from our Read Along sessions as words needing our special attention for better pronunciation. You may want to create your own collection of words from reading with your class or modify the list I have provided. What list you have is of no consequence, what matters is that you have a list of special words difficult for the Chinese mouth. In a typical two school-year period, we revise our list at least six times and keep adding and removing words as the need arises. We refer to this word sheet in most class sessions as an integral part of improving our pronunciation.

6. Elaboration: Some stories contain longer, multi-syllable words that are too difficult to catch by just repeating them once. I am sometimes surprised at some of the big words used in readers, but these are good for stretching the student's ability, and I stop and use these longer words to teach articulation, syllables, phonics, pronunciation quirks, and other things. I also use such words to teach exaggerated articulation, sounding out each syllable and going over it several times with them. This teaches them to use phonetics to sound out a new word on their own.

7. Participation: I often have the students read one paragraph and then we go over the pronunciation together when I read the paragraph. I have a different student read each paragraph and then critique words that are mispronounced. I may add the mispronounced word to *The Word Sheet* and have a drill on the word or ask for synonyms.

Be prepared to have HC students tell you that Read Along is not as effective in helping them learn English as discussion times. High comprehension students have a preference for discussion because they feel it's a better way to practice their English than Read Along because it is closer to real conversation. However, as teachers we must make a distinction between students' preference and what we know to be the best method for achieving our goals of speech quality. High comprehenders may enjoy discussions more, but without Read Along, we have lost the LC's because they don't have the skills that are needed to express themselves well in English during discussions. High comprehenders must understand that when they are in a class with LC's, we must all give and take a little. If I have too much discussion in a mixed class of low and high comprehenders, the low comprehenders are left out. In addition, during a discussion, only one student can talk with the teacher at a time, but in Read Along *all of the students* are talking along with the teacher at the same time. Read Along includes every student rather than just a few. It is important that every student is speaking a great deal in class, and Read Along accomplishes that.

A class of 32 students usually has an average ECLS of about 5.3 to 5.5. The top student in one of my classes at the time of this writing is 7.1. The bottom comprehender is a 4.9. This is more than two full points (or levels) of difference in comprehension between my high comprehenders and my low comprehenders. That is a big span of difference in comprehension with which the teacher must deal. When I am using a teaching method such as discussion that benefits the high comprehenders, I am not doing much for the LC. When I use a method of teaching in which my LC's can fully participate, I am doing little for the HC. As teachers, what do we do in such a case to make sure all of our students are well served?

My suggestion is to keep your techniques varied and diverse in an attempt to reach everyone. Use the Read Along to get everyone's participation. Then pick words out of the text of your readers and write them on the board and challenge students to construct sentences using the new words. Finally, hold a discussion on the outcome of the story. When you use multiple methods (e.g., word studies, drills, discussions) along with Read Along, you have managed to span the whole spectrum of comprehension in your class.

The truth is that Read Along (as well as Talk Along and Follow Along) helps the high comprehenders more than they realize because many of them have pronunciation problems, and these exercises, if carefully entered into by students, will help their pronunciation immensely on a subconscious level.

More About Discussions

Discussions are certainly one of the best ways to develop conversational English, but shyness is a big factor in having good participation in class discussions. You can help your shy students to open up more in class through several methods. I follow these rules: First, never openly embarrass a shy student. A self-conscious student doesn't like to make mistakes in front of the other students or to be singled out. Secondly, relaxed students, including the shy, feel free to speak out if they are doing it all together. At first I had a strong rule that required showing hands to get permission to speak. I dropped that rule when I discovered that the freedom to speak out will evoke more response. I don't want to discourage spontaneous speech or enthusiasm. After the rule was lifted, I could see even my shy students muttering something. So now I use a very effective tactic. I let them speak out together and then when they do, I go to their desk and hold a conversation with them using the basic, *Who, What, Why, Where,* and *When* questions. While you're talking with that one student, other students will start chiming in with their two cents. I will then go to the shy student and only ask if he or she agrees with that last answer. The student only needs to respond with a yes or no. I note that he or she is *right!* Little by little you will see your shy students develop better participation. With time on your side and paying special attention to your special students, you'll have most of the class involved before you know it ... and before they know it!

Let me share an example of effective discussion technique. President Hu suddenly made a speech at the outset of the Severe Acute Respiratory Syndrome, or SARS, epidemic and contradicted other Chinese news sources that were assuring the nation that the SARS problem was under control. In an act of good leadership, he stated clearly with Mr. Wen Jinbao, the Premier, that the epidemic was serious and could interfere with China's "economy, its national image and social stability" if it was not dealt with quickly. I read the report taken from China's news agencies to the class. I asked the following general question: *Should Mr. Hu and Mr. Wen tell the nation SARS is not under control if it is not?*

Of course it was my opinion that the answer should be *yes*, because the people would become more cautious about using preventative methods against the deadly and contagious disease if they were told the truth, but it was surprising how many students said, *no*, they should not tell the truth. Now we were beginning to see all the elements of a good discussion:

- A current event on everyone's mind

- A difference of opinion

- The opportunity to teach an important life lesson.

I followed up the general question with questions that required the class to look more deeply into the dilemma: *What could be the outcome of their honesty?* The honest comments could save lives. *What character traits do we see in these two men?* Mr. Hu said he "feared for the masses." This reveals his concern for the people.

The discussion was hot! In one class the majority said he should *not* have told the people the truth. We had a big discussion about *why* he should not have. I then asked the class to follow the outcome of such a policy to its disastrous conclusion. In the end we were all of the same mind and had a deeper respect for our national leaders. The topic pulled all of the students into the discussion. Discussions are most educational and beneficial when the participation is high. Discussion teaches students to answer moral questions honestly and conditions them to experience the good outcome of being honest, but above all, students are unconsciously improving their conversational powers of English!

Discussions from current events or hot news items (except materials that advocate personal political or religious views) draw the student into an interest-oriented discussion. Discussions on the reading materials in workbooks deal with routine matters, but news articles that grab the interest and evoke opinion are excellent materials for getting a good discussion heated up. You know a discussion is going well when some of your students start cutting out in Chinese to express their views. I call them back to English, but inside I have a good laugh, enjoying their enthusiasm.

There are many readers (textbooks) with good discussion materials available in any State Publishing House bookstore. The *Oral Workshop Discussion* distributed by the Foreign Language Teaching and Research Press is 430 pages in length and contains 35 lessons. Each lesson contains two or three reading selections and special study sections including notes, phrases and related words and expressions, Chinese sayings and slogans, and a related picture (cartoon). It's an excellent reader for Read Along and for a discussion to follow which gives us the chance to then have an open discussion after the story is read together. This manual is also replete with ideas and methods of relating to the topics. It is in itself a manual for classroom procedure as you teach the content.

There are many readers out there that can be used to do the same thing. All you have to do is visit any bookstore in any major city and you will find shelves laden with excellent workbooks and manuals. I have found many short novels available in the bookstores including such classics as *Heidi* and *Black Beauty*. There are many others, and it would be a good thing to become familiar with what the bookstores carry. You may have the freedom to choose your own reader with the permission of the Foreign Language Dean and the Foreign Affairs Office Director. They will need to have the title of the reader and the publisher for approval. If you can get a sample copy to them, that would be ideal.

Chapter Eight
Talk Along and Follow Along

I seldom give a solo lecture in my Oral English classes. Instead, I have the class follow me, repeating after me everything I say to them. This is called "Talk Along." Sometimes when a story gets very dramatic or it's affecting their thinking, their voices will slowly trail off into silence because they are absorbed in what I am saying. When they fall into this silence, I allow them to remain silent and listen. Communication is, after all, listening and not speaking. When they lapse into that silent listening mode, I know they are absorbed in listening. This usually lasts a brief time only and indicates a deep impression. They usually pick up again after we pass over the part that is absorbing their thoughts, and we go on normally with the lecture.

I often give six-day weather reports the first thing in class from the Internet – www.wunderground.com – and type in the name of your city anywhere in the world. My students have learned that when I am speaking, they are to follow me. When I start a lecture, I usually begin with the instruction, "Follow me." They know they are to keep their eyes peeled on me and repeat every word I say. Every few weeks I give them a little pep talk about getting the most out of their Oral English class by carefully following my speech and watching my face. I use different approaches each time. This helps them to remain focused.

The Talk Along method differs from the Read Along exercises in that during the Read Along, the student has to read and repeat, and it takes more effort. In Talk Along, the reading component has been dropped, and the student can concentrate on listening very carefully to the sound of my words and then repeating them. This allows them to focus more on the sound of the teacher's pronunciation.

The Talk Along method also gives me a chance to visit each student by walking around the classroom while I speak extemporaneously to the class. In this method, you are able to go from student to student and from one side of the classroom to the other, making eye contact with each student. Unlike the Read Along, the teacher does not have to keep attention tuned to the reader or a piece of paper. If I come near a student, I can listen for incorrectly pronounced words. The students love that closeness and the attention they are getting. If I hear a student not using the correct pronunciation, I repeat the word again and again with the whole class following while I work with that one student. After you do this a few times, the students get adjusted to the method and know it's a word that needs their special attention and effort, and they follow carefully no matter how many times I repeat the word. These students want to learn correct pronunciation. If they know you love them and you want to help them, they'll follow you to the moon!

Content of Talk Along Lectures

In teaching Oral English, we have the opportunity to choose from a range of material that will help students learn proper English language articulation. That's the first objective, but as we have pointed out elsewhere, we should also carefully prepare good materials for lecture content. The two best subjects would probably be character development and current events. Current events could include many subjects from technology and the sciences to the current big news item. The important thing is to have good substance to your lecture content, so the student is learning good life principles along with his speech skills. I incorporate character-building topics such as ethics in business, protocol, etiquette, good manners, personal hygiene, and life principles such as coping with heartbreak and disappointments in life. China is one of the few nations where the central government advocates and legislates the importance of character education. The Chinese government, for example, has been criticized by foreign countries for controlling the Internet and other forms of entertainment that corrupt the character of youth. Every teacher who stands in a Chinese classroom should support the Chinese government by teaching life values that will build the character of the next generation as well as the economy of the New China. My first objective as an Oral English teacher is English speech skills, but the content of my teaching materials is my second great concern. I try to assure that my lectures have good moral substance that helps to build character.

Follow Along

Follow Along is a third way of interactive reading with your students. Talk Along is when the class follows your lecture as you're speaking extemporaneously, but when I am reading from material they do not have in hand, we call that Follow Along. I often bring material clipped from newspapers or magazines to which I know they will well relate and have the class Follow Along as I read the article. I did this daily through the SARS epidemic to keep the students well informed about the crisis. If you have only one copy and want to use it for a hand out sheet, you can have copies made in your language department office, or share it orally by using the article as a Follow Along, having them repeat as you read each word or phrase.

During Follow Along, the student closely follows every word the teacher is saying, concentrating on the pronunciation of each word. We stop frequently, giving me an opportunity to explain the meaning of new words. This is another great opportunity to use pantomime to demonstrate word definitions. I also sometimes call on a couple of students to come up and act something out with me. It's always a lot of fun for the students. We often get some good laughs out of it. For example, once I wanted to demonstrate the word *embrace*. I called one of the boys to come up and stand at one end of the classroom in the front. I went to the other side and told the class that I saw in the crowded rail station an old comrade with whom I fought in the revolution. He saved my life in a very bloody battle! He was now in his seventies – which brought a laugh because this boy was twenty. I watched him in the crowd, and I thought it was my old comrade, but I was not sure. Fifty years had passed since I last saw him! Finally I decided to call out his name. When I did he wheeled around and looked into my eyes. His face lit up! We walked toward each other with our arms outstretched (and I had the boy walk toward me with his arms open).

We walked into each other's arms, crying on each other's shoulder, crying out, *"Comrade! Comrade!"*

By now the class was cheering and laughing as we embraced each other. Then I explained to students that we *embraced*, and gave them some synonyms such as *hug* and *hold*.

Pantomiming and little skits are good methods for getting across the subtle meanings of new words and improving vocabulary. Some will remember such scenes the rest of their lives!

Chapter Nine
Secondary Objectives and Miscellaneous Exercises

Vocabulary

While this skill is not our main concern – pronunciation is – any development of English skills will need to concern itself with vocabulary. We inevitably will learn new words throughout the course of our Read Along, Talk Along, and Follow Along exercises. When we encounter new words, there are exercises and procedures that can turn these into useful parts of students' vocabularies. If you don't treat new words effectively, they will simply evaporate into the thin air of forgetfulness. To reach our vocabulary goals we should approach each new word with these three steps in mind.

    1. Familiarization: You must first familiarize your students with a new word or phrase. You can do this by having them approach the word on several levels: hearing, writing, and pronouncing the word. When we meet a new word, we want to know all about that word by dividing its syllables and noting its spelling and perhaps even its etymology (origin). It's like meeting people for the first time and becoming acquainted with them. You are learning about them to establish a good close friendship. You will take notes on every new word and then write all you can learn about that word in a brief paragraph upon your first few meetings. You will want to add many of these new words to your vocabulary by trying to use them on the same day you meet them. Sometimes I introduce a new word by writing it out on the board without saying it and then ask the class to sound it out and say it for me. After we learn to pronounce the word correctly, I may tell a short story with the new word as the theme. Upon hearing and learning a new word once, it may be lodged in the memory, but it does not mean the student knows how to use it and include it in his/her vocabulary. Familiarization has happened when the word has become familiar to us.

2. Definition: Definition occurs when the word's full meaning is finally mentally imbedded. Asking the students to use the new word in a sentence will help them to get a good grasp of the meaning. Having the students look the word up in a dictionary and using the new word in sentences will also help bring the learning to this level. Once I introduce a new word, I write it on the left page of my class diary for that class day. In the next class I write the word on the board, and we review it again and use all of our new words in sentences. In a week or two I will write sentences on the blackboard, leaving blanks to fill in with the new words. It's best to call on one student at a time to fill in the correct word on the board, rather than allow open response. Defining has happened when the word is lodged in the mind and is ready to be used on command.

3. Application and Beyond: This level of learning is achieved when we are able to correctly and extemporaneously apply – use – what we have learned. We have reached this level when a word becomes available to us on demand, a part of our oral armory. Reaching the third level of learning is when we have permanently added the word to our personal lexicons. I am careful to choose the words I want them to add to their vocabulary. They should be words they can use daily in normal conversation. I want students to be able to express themselves fluently when holding a common conversation. Specialized words that are not commonly used every day can be added later, but the words they will use every day must be learned first. There are some words we meet in readers that they do not need to spend time learning because they are words they will seldom use, such as *forensic* or *kink*. I introduce them to such words but spend the bulk of time on words they will need and be able to use in their everyday lives.

The three levels of learning described here closely parallel the first three levels of the taxonomy of learning behaviors identified by Benjamin Bloom, a recognized authority in educational psychology.

Starters

Helping the students form complete sentences in their own minds enables them to think in English and become more self-confident in conversing with another English speaking person. It is important to teach phrases that will help to start them out in an English conversation. I call these phrases *starters*. This strategy will work well in long or short blocks of time. If you have ten minutes to go until class ends, you may want to put a *starter* up on the board and let students exercise themselves in those last few minutes before you release them from class. Learning these phrases will help students to begin the process of putting words together into fluent sentences to boost confidence and create real conversational skills.

Here are a few examples which only serve as primers. You can produce scores and scores of other *starters*.

Could you please tell me the time?

I write the first two or three words on the board and ask them to finish the phrase in various ways. For example:

Could you please ... move over a little ?

Could you ... hand that to me, please ?

Could you... see that?

Could you... do that for me?

Or,

What do you ... think of that?

What do you ... do there?

What do ... they do for a living?

What do ... they like to do?

You write the words printed in italics and then let the students finish the starters in various ways.

Here are more two/three word starters to let them finish in their own words:

Are you . . .

   ...sure?

   ...healthy?

   ...leaving now?

   ...able?

   ...returning home?

More starters would be:

Can you ...	*Does that ...*
Do you think ...	*That is a ...*
I believe ...	*Should we ...*
Will they ...	*It's probably ...*
I will be ...	*They are ...*
It's a ...	*Let's ...*
It ...	*Can ...*
I ...	*Perhaps ...*
Its ...	*Could ...*
We ...	*You ...*
Today I ...	*I think ...*
Tomorrow is ...	*I wish ...*

Tip: When I ask questions in class, I want complete sentences and not one word as an answer. This helps students to form complete sentences in English.

An example: *How is she acting when she stomps out of the room?*

Wrong answer: *angry*

Right answer: *She is acting angry.*

It is important to teach them to give their answers in complete sentences.

The Word Hunt

Another good exercise is the word hunt. It's a vocabulary builder in every way.

Begin by writing a rather long word on the board. Be sure it's an interesting word, because the first thing you will do is help students sound out the word by syllables and then explain the meaning. It may be a word they will not use that much in their vocabulary at this point, but it should nevertheless be interesting to them. The real reason for familiarizing them with this big new word is to tap their brain to discover what kind of vocabulary they have.

Hand out a piece of paper to individual students and have them place their regular header at the top including their English name, date, and class number across the top from left to right. Then have them draw a line under that header and write the big new word from the board across the top of their paper stretching from the right to left edges if possible.

Now you will tell them they have 15 minutes to find as many other English words in that one word as possible, using only the letters in that word. Here are some examples of words you can use. *catastrophic*, *extemporaneously*, or *conditionally*. Taking the word *extemporaneously*, we see there are no –*i*'s and no –*k*'s. So, they cannot use words with those letters in them. Also be sure to advise them that they cannot use a duplicate of a letter contained in the word. For example, they cannot use the word "*memory*" with two –*m*'s out of the word *extemporaneously*, which contains only one –*m*.

This exercise will reveal to the teacher which students have the best vocabulary in their class. Many times it's not your high comprehenders that produce the longest list of words! One boy in my class had an average comprehension of 5.8 but found 70 words in *extemporaneously*. My high comprehender in that class had a 7.1 comprehension and found only 35 words. Again, it is one of those many conundrums that make these non-graded tests so interesting and helpful to us as teachers to understand our students' skills. I will do only two or three word hunts a year with paper scores. The students enjoy it, and it gives you as a teacher some good insight. The word hunt can be carried out in various ways.

For example, it can be a formal written class activity. Hand out papers to all of the students and give them a set time to find as many words as possible. Then I appoint a team of 2 students to make a complete list of the total of different words from all papers and report in the next class. I do this in all of my classes and then declare the winning class and the student with the highest number of original words. Or, the word hunt can be a smaller, less formal instructional unit. With a few minutes remaining at the end of class you can write a word on the board and let them call out the words as you (or a student) write them on the board. I sometimes will divide a classroom into two teams, have two students come to the board, and see how many different words each side can find in 5 minutes. They really get into it, and it develops vocabulary and speech skills.

This exercise is also recommended as a 5 to 10 minute activity when your class time is almost finished, but you don't really have time to start another project. I have a conviction that I am being paid to give my students full 50-minute classes every time we come together. Their parents have sacrificed to give them a college education, and I am obligated to assure that my students receive two fifty minute class periods per class session each time we meet. Starters and the Word Hunt are two exercises that sharpen students' learning skills and also help me to put all of my class time to good use if I have a few minutes to spare after I have finished my lessons.

Word Drill

I use the Word Drill often and in all of the other methods of teaching such as in Read Along and Talk Along, but especially while working with *The Word Sheet* – see the following chapter – when we discover a hang-up in the pronunciation of a particular syllable in a word. The drill helps me locate the students who are having serious pronunciation problems. Then I work with them one-on-one to help them iron out their difficulties.

You can use the Word Drill in several different ways and at different times. If a word we find while in discussion or in responsive speech is sounding bad, I suddenly call for a Word Drill. It can be a sudden, spontaneous change in methodology, which will always wake the students up. Before starting the Word Drill, I always work with them as a group, pronouncing the word correctly and breaking it up into syllables. I give them all a chance to become familiar with the correct pronunciation. I want them to improve the sound and make corrections themselves. I call for the word to be pronounced in unison several times. Then I call for a Word Drill. This is an opportunity for each student to interact with the teacher. Word Drills always put the class into a high alert mode. Students know they're going to have to take part. Sometimes I start in the front row, sometimes I start in the back, and sometimes I give a random drill.

I say, "*Now let's have a Word Drill on 'curl,'*" a difficult word with both an *–r* and an *–l* in it.

I repeat the word several times. Then I gesture with my hand to the student who will start the drill, and we move across the front row and then to the next row and across. One by one each student pronounces the word, and I can immediately tell who has mastered the sound and who is still having troubles.

Sometimes I use a random drill pattern, going from student to student to pronounce the drill word, and I don't go from front to back or back to front. I jump around from one side of the class to the other side and from front to back, gesturing to the student I want to give the word we're working on. They really start practicing then, thinking they could be next. Anything that activates them is good for learning extemporaneous oral English. I sometimes call for just one row to drill, or starting at the front, I move straight back in a line from front to rear. I like to hear my class go into "alert and practice" mode, where I hear them mumbling all over the classroom to prepare for their turn. The drill and pronunciation exercise demands the students' participation and involvement.

In order to assure that this pressure is productive and not intimidating, I am sure to emphasize again that making mistakes is a big part of learning. We are all making similar mistakes, and we are learning by listening to each other. After the drill, I analyze their speech for them, pointing out the mispronunciations. The same errors usually appear over and over. We have a lot of fun when we do this drill because we are all listening for the strange ways the word is pronounced. As I have emphasized before, it's advisable not to use an open class drill in freshmen classes until after a few weeks into the first semester, giving them time to become acquainted with each other. After five to six weeks, they don't mind making mistakes with others around. I learned this lesson after losing two good students from my classes. If they are among friends, it's not going to embarrass them, but this waiting period is the best rule for those few who have sensitive temperaments and come from backgrounds that make them shy about such things. After the getting acquainted period, they will enjoy their mistakes. What will be perfectly acceptable after six weeks could be embarrassing and cause them to lose face with their strange classmates if it happens in the first or second week. This is a very important caution to the foreign teacher.

Noun Search in Pictures

Another exercise that is good for students of English is the Noun Search. In readers and material we use in Oral English, there are often illustrations with some detail. For example, in our *Oral Workshop: Discussion* readers there is a cartoon illustration of a man visiting the doctor (page 23). There are many objects in the picture that make it a good drill on nouns for the students. They can point out the names of the objects in the picture, practicing their vocabulary and their pronunciation. You can also have copies made of an interesting picture and do a Noun Search and weave a Talk Along story around the picture with the students.

I use Oxford University materials. In the overhead transparency binder, they have excellent colored illustrations of scenes under different topics and many of these detailed picture drawings are rich with objects to make a Noun Search as well as other discussion possibilities. The imagination is all it takes to make a great oral lesson from a good illustration.

Chapter Ten
Correcting Chronic Mispronunciations

Earlier in the manual, I discussed The Word Sheet, which is made up of words that are especially difficult to pronounce. This is the primary tool I use for working on words and sounds that are particularly difficult for Chinese students. Let's take a look at the various parts of this list here. The document contains four parts, each aimed at helping students concentrate their pronunciation efforts.

Part 1 contains a list of difficult words. (See *Figure 10.1*, **The Four High Hurdles of Pronunciation,** near the end of this chapter.) You can create your own list of difficult words for The Word Sheet. Simply isolate words difficult to pronounce by discovering them in your students' speech recitations during any class activity. Once you have isolated a problematic word, it should be added to your list of difficult words. That list then becomes the basis of your efforts to improve their pronunciation, allowing you to return directly to the problem words whenever you need to work on pronunciation. I have isolated about sixty such words on my Word Sheet.

Students tend to love this list because they know it represents their goal of good pronunciation. They feel that if they can tackle this list, they will have made a major breakthrough. All students participate in this pronunciation exercise enthusiastically! It is a challenge to them, and they attack the sounds with real zeal.

In the second part of The Word Sheet, Understanding Your Oral Dilemmas (*Figure 10.2*), we name the seven most difficult sounds for the Chinese student to master. There are other sounds that are also tricky, but these are the most complicated, and we have isolated them in order to concentrate our efforts on replacing these oral enemies of good English with correct pronunciation. Because of individual differences, there are going to be some students who have extreme difficulty with some sounds with which most other students have no trouble. You may want to improve on this list, but this gives you a start in the right direction.

Probably the two most difficult sounds for the Chinese mouth to form are \l\ in the final position, as in *tall,* and the \r\ in medial and final positions, as in *world* and *where*. But there is a phenomenon that you will discover and be able to use to correct the problem of the final \l\. I was puzzled because students could easily pronounce an English word with a beginning –l but could not pronounce one with a final –l. So I developed a remedial activity that I call the reversed word exercise that is explained in detail in *Figure 10.2*. After I made this discovery and explained it to the class, Roy, a first year student, came to me one afternoon and explained to me that the reason for this phenomenon was that they did not have any Chinese words that ended with -l, but they had many words that began with -l. That solved the mystery. So, this *is* the one big pronunciation hurdle of them all to overcome, to get that -l pronounced at the end of a word as easily as it is pronounced at the beginning of a word. It's not going to be easy, but the reversed word exercise detailed in *Figure 10.2* is one of the best methods to accomplish this. For the \r\ and other difficult sounds, additional exercises are prescribed, including labial and lingual awareness and muscle control.

Part 3 details another option to consider, Arbitrary Phonetic Alternative Spelling, that is very effective in helping students overcome their roadblocks to intelligible pronunciation. This intervention is also explained at length in *Figure 10.3*.

Part 4 (See *Figure 10.4*) is the "Struggle" page that lists the words with two consonants, a soft sound following a hard consonant together, the last one (soft sound) being an –*l*, making it extremely difficult for the Chinese mouth to form, as in *puddle*. This page also supplies activities with words containing similar sounds such as *shall* and *shell*.

"Pinglish" is a word I have coined identifying many of the unwanted accents in the speech of Chinese students of English. It implies half Pinyin and half English. However, much of the mispronunciation I hear in my students is not attributable to a Chinese accent as many teachers may think. It is caused by what I call the "alphabet syndrome." You may not know this, but your Chinese students have been wrestling with competing alphabets throughout their education, for they must learn 3 Latin alphabets by the time they pass through high school! First, they learn the Pinyin Latin Alphabet – or PLA – with its peculiar pronunciations. Later, they are taught the International Phonetic Alphabet – or IPA – which is another Latin alphabet with a second set of different pronunciations peculiar to that alphabet. Finally, they are taught the classic English Latin Alphabet – or ELA – with yet a third set of different alphabetical pronunciations. It's quite a tangle! Exposure to three different Latin alphabets with three different sets of sounds for many of the letters in each compounds the task of learning English for the Chinese student. Most of the mispronunciations in English are not "Chinglish," but "Pinglish" accents. The sounds they can and cannot pronounce are from Pinyin. This is why they say "ash**e**med" instead of "ashamed," for example.

I am a bit of a crank on this phenomenon, regarding the teaching of the three alphabets as superfluous and a bit senseless. It causes several linguistic conflicts including variations in pronunciation that become confusing to the student. The IPA will not be used in the real world. Surely learning its alphabetic symbols is one of the reasons most Chinese students of English cannot write in English cursive and have very little knowledge of the basics of classic English letters and writing. My university students write in a script that is half cursive and half IPA and don't even know how to write the English alphabet in beautiful English script. It seems that if we are learning English, we should stick with one form of the English language and that would be the English the student will be using entirely upon graduation, the classic English alphabet. My students have corrected me when I've written on the board while teaching, telling me I have written a word with the wrong letters. When I ask them to come to the board and write it correctly, they come and write the word with a combination of classic English letters and IPA letters! If they were to concentrate on the ultimate classic English alphabet that students will use in the real world once they leave college, it would avoid much frustration and struggle.

Figure 10.1

The Four High Hurdles of Pronunciation

(All pronunciation exercises are based on American accent.)

1	2	3	4
usually	puddle	rural	length
ashamed	actually	fulfill	world
cookies	casually	oversized	poll
wall(s)	practically	realized	while
oral	dull	delicious	whistle
bulb	bugs	discuss	violence
try	principle	disgusted	order
all	explain	needle	eagle
quilt	thanks	noodles	measure
slightly	really	could	smile
south	bulk	grove	couple
quiet	bowl	groove	angel
result	twinkle	quarrel	model
desire	schedule	shall	huddle
required	sharp	tell	barrel
pull	curl	whirl	delight
quarry	rule	lungs	old

Figure 10.2

Understanding Your Oral Dilemmas

The seven sounds that vex the tongue and defy our resolve given in the order of their strength:

1. \l\ All English words ending with -*l* or having an -*l* in the middle of the word.

Ending with – *l*:

The final - *l* as in *ball, call, tall, shall*

An – *l* in the middle:

The medial –*l* as in *world, old, cold, million*

Incorrect:

Pronouncing –*l* as a –*w* or as *aw*\

Pronouncing *tall* as *taw*\

Pronouncing *share* as *shay-owe*\

Correction:

Learn to use the tongue, not the lips to pronounce the -*l*.

Phenomena:

You can pronounce a word that starts with - *l* but not ending with - *l*.

Exercise:

You can pronounce the –*l* in *let* because the word starts with –*l*, but you find it extremely difficult to pronounce the same –*l* when it is at the end of a word.

Here is how you can learn to pronounce your –*l*'s when the word ends with –*l*:

Repeat the word *l-e-t*\, *l-e-t*\, *l-e-t*\ slowly. Now reverse the word and you have *tell*\. Practice starting the word *tell* and then start the word *let* slowly. By running these two words together *telll-lllet*\, \ *telll-lllet*\, you are learning to place the good sounding –*l* at the end of *tell*. Now do the same thing with *call* and *lack, calll-lllack,* until you have the good sounding –*l* on *all*.

You can use many words in reverse to achieve the proper –*l* sound in words ending in –*l*. In fact, you can do it with a combination of words whether they sound similar or not.

Example: *talll-llletter*\ *or* *parallelll-lllook*\

We have transformed the pronunciation skills of scores of our students with this simple oral exercise. By joining two words, the first that ends with the difficult –*l*, and then the second word that begins with the easier to pronounce –*l*, and then running two -l's together in the middle \tellll-llllet\ can make both –l's sound good. Finally, after you have the bad –l converted to the right sounding –l, you can say only \tellll\ and drop the \et\ in *let*. This is a simple exercise and really works wonders in getting rid of the bad "-*aw*-sounding" –l.

2.\r\ Words using \r\ are especially troublesome when the \r\ is combined with another one of these difficult letters to sound in this list.

Incorrect:

Pronouncing \r\ as a –w, saying \whay-owe\ instead of *where* and \scay-ode\ instead of *scared*, and especially difficult when combined with another one of these difficult sounds listed here such as in *world*, \woe-wode\, where you have an –r and –l together, pronouncing the –r with the lips instead of with the tongue.

Correction:

Learn to use the tongue and eliminate the use of the lips.

Exercise:

Tighten the lips above your teeth and speak, not using your lips, and paying special attention to words with -r in them. Practice the sound of the -r without the lips.

3. \a\ or the long –a as in *aye*. Words using –a are pronounced as \eh\ instead of \aye\. The cause of this is the lingering letter sounds taught in Pinyin and the International

Alphabets, which have sounds different from the classical Latin alphabet pronunciation.

Incorrect:

Pronouncing *ashamed* as *ashemed*\ and all long –*a* sounds with the *eh*\ instead of *aye*\.

Correction:

Learn to pronounce the classical Latin alphabet –*a* properly as a long –*a,* as in *say, may, Stacy, play.*

Exercise:

Make a list of words using the long –*a,* or take the words in the list above with long –*a* and practice them. Get one well and then apply the same sounds to the other words with long –*a,* as in *ashamed, claim, tame, lame,* etc.

4. \i\ As in – *a*, there are three sounds in – *i*. Our problem is with the long – *i* that rhymes with eye, as it is with the long –*a*. Difficult words are *sight, kite, right, pile, tile,* and so forth.

Incorrect:

Pronouncing *kite* as *kit* or *Kate*.

Correction:

Familiarize yourself with the correct sound of the long – *a* in the words in our *Secrets to Better English – SBE –* list above. Onc or two words gotten perfectly are best. Pronounce words with the long –i putting the *eye* in place of the long –i as in this example: *bite* \beyete\; *tired* \teyered\; *kind* \keyend\.

Exercise:

Start practicing the sound using only one or two words that may be the most difficult for you. Get them perfectly and then attack all of the others and they will be easier to defeat if you master the sound in one word first. Listen to a taped narration or English radio and watch for the words using the long –a, and then repeat them.

5. \o\ This is one of the more complex sounds because of the variant ways of pronouncing \o\ and especially in the double –o (oo) forms. Sometimes the two –o's together in a word have two sounds such as in *cooperation*. The sound of double –o in *cook* and *took* is different than that in the double –o in *zoom* and *broom*. The most difficult sound for us is in *cookie* and *book*.

Incorrect:

Saying \cokie\ instead of *cookie*, and \buke\ instead of *book*.

Correction:

Carefully listen to the slight differences between the sounds of *book* and *loom*.

Exercise:

Make two lists, one with the \oo\ as in *room* and the other with the \oo\ as in *book*. You must familiarize yourself with these two subtle differences in sound, and then practice them from the list you build.

6. \sh\ shshsh In Chinese we have the \s\ sound but more hushed and hissy than the English –sh. This, by the way, is actually a word listed in some recent dictionaries as an English word spelled as we have it here. Many English words need a clear and distinctive \shshsh\ sound to be understood.

Incorrect:

Hissing and missing. Few students have mastered this sound and still use the hissing sound, or the sound is hardly audible. Not \si\ but \she\; not \tsake\, but \shake\.

Correction:

The \sh\ is a consonant digraph and like most digraphs has a sound that is totally different from the usual sounds of the letters *(–s* and *–h)* by themselves. The new sound is a voiceless sound, a fricative that is made by forcing air from the front of the mouth through slightly open teeth while at the same time forming with the lips the \sh\ sound as in *shoes, shine,* or *sheet*. In the pronunciation, one first hears the unvoiced rush of air, and then the voiced vowel and consonant sounds. With a little practice, the unvoiced and voiced sounds can be blended together to create intelligible words beginning with the \sh\ sound.

Exercise:

Practice the above instruction until you get a loud and clear \shshsh\ sound. Once you achieve the sound, apply it to the word or words that use the sound and **keep the volume up** (shall, shoot, share, rash, shush).

Note:

If you open your dictionary to the words beginning with –sh, you will have a long list of words to help you practice the \sh\ sound with your class. A good audio English dictionary can be a helpful tool and can play a big part in helping your students with pronunciation.

7. \zh\ zhzhzh This is easy to accomplish because it's very close to the \shshsh\ sound above. But, it is one of the sounds most non-native students of English have a great deal of trouble with. It's usually very weak and hardly audible. Also, the Pinyin sound in the name, *Rang,* and the Chinese currency, *RMB,* have the \zhzh\ sound in them.

Incorrect:

This sound is usually missing or replaced with the \w\ again as in *usually* which is too often pronounced \yoo-wal-lee\. The –s, \zhzh\, sound is silenced and missing. When the –s is pronounced, there is sometimes a tendency toward the sharp \s\ rather than \zhu\. This is an important sound that we must master.

Correction:

To master this sound, first master the \shshsh\ above and then simply add the sound of the voice with the \shsh\ and you will get the \zhzhzh\ sound.

Exercise:

Follow the instructions in Number 6 above and then start using the voice box with the \shsh\ and you will have the \zhzh\ sound. This sound is important because it is one of the sounds of the -s and is found in many words such as *casually, usually,* and *occasion.*

Actually, there is a third -s sound that is pronounced as \z\ as in *pause, cause,* and *raise.* But this \zhzh\ sound is the difficult one to master.

Figure 10.3

Arbitrary Phonetic Alternative Spelling – APAS

Students wanting to improve their pronunciation outside the classroom can use this very effective classroom exercise. It has been a great help to many of my students of English. The teacher writes out the correctly spelled, difficult word on the board. It can be used for any difficult word depending only on the imagination of the teacher. Under the correct word start writing the same word with several arbitrary phonetic spellings that make it easier for the students to sound out.

APAS goes far to help correct mispronunciations. This method does require some creative work on the part of the Oral English teacher, but it can be a big help when the mispronunciation is chronic.

For example, the little word *try* is a big bad pronunciation problem. The student always wants to say, *twy*, which strikes the native English ear as baby talk. The Chinese mouth wants to substitute the \r\ with a \w\ and \l\ because it sounds similar when used as a substitute in words where they cannot pronounce the –l or the –r. It's the consonant blend –tr that is most difficult in addition to the unstressed syllable that follows the double consonant, as in *puddle. (See Figure 10.4, # 1, for an explanation of unstressed syllables.)* These are the most difficult pronunciation problems Chinese students have, but they can be effectively corrected by writing the word on the board in different phonetic forms, e.g., *ter-rie* or *tu-wry*. It works like magic with most students! Any difficult word can usually be corrected with a phonetically spelled sound-alike.

Simple words like *the* and *they* have the difficult \th\ digraph (a pair of letters making one sound) factor which is hard for the Chinese mouth. The digraph is the sound that results when you put together 2 consonants that do not retain their original individual sounds, as in *–ch, –wh*, etc.

But these are comparatively easy to correct compared to such words as *puddle, rural,* and *usually.*

For *world* they want to say \woe-wode\, \wode\, or \ward\. To get students to say *world* correctly, I spell it phonetically as *wur-uld*. As soon as they are saying the word correctly, go immediately back to the correct spelling of the word and have them use the word in a sentence. I always keep the word correctly spelled and underlined on the board when I write out the arbitrary phonetic alternatives. When you see them looking around at each other with big grins on their faces, then you know they are pleased with themselves and saying it right.

After they get rid of the wrong pronunciation, I teach them to speak the word quickly. You can create these phonetic spellings arbitrarily and form them in any combination of syllables you think best to get the word sounding right then go back to the correct spelling. They can correct *world* much easier than the \tr\ and the \dəl\.

Here are some other examples using APAS:

Puddle: *pudd-dull* or *pu-dull*

The key is to first master the word *dull.*

Call: *k-all* The key is to master the word *all.*

Desire: *Dee-zie-yer* seems to make it easier.

Figure 10.4

The Three Big Struggles of Mouth Control

Complied by Dr. Bill Burkett, teacher of Oral and Business English

1. Overcoming the double consonant syndrome or mispronunciation of words with unstressed syllables. The tendency to say **BU**-go\ instead of **BU**-gle\.

Many words containing medial double consonant letters such as *puddle* have the stress or emphasis on the first syllable, e.g., **PUD**-dle\. Stress is simply the intensity with which you utter a word or a part of a word – a syllable. When a syllable is stressed, it is more intense or more pronounced than the unstressed syllable.

In words with double consonants, unstressed syllables such as *ble*\, *dle*\, and *tle*\ are usually represented by the \ə1\, pronounced *uhl*\. For example, *bubble*: **BUB**-ə1\; *little*: **LIT**-ə1\; and *bottle*: **BOT**-ə1\.

More examples:

nibble, cuddle, struggle, cattle, rattle

In words without double consonants, unstressed syllables such as \ble\, \kle\, and \tle\ usually represent the consonant sound in the syllable + \ə1\. For example, *able:* **A**-bə1\, *ankle:* **ANG**-kə1\, and *title:* **TI**-tə1\.

Additional examples:

bungle, curdle, hurdle, shackle, tackle, trouble

2. Eliminating the *w*\ and *ow*\ from all words with –r, and –l.

3. Pairs of words that sound the same except for one sound difference, such as *shall* and *shell*; *sell* and *sale*; *pal* and *pail*.

Chapter Eleven
Teaching the Whole Student

As a teacher of Oral English, your job is to do more than simply help with conversant English and pronunciation. Your students are not just speakers, they are also people with concerns, fears, and struggles all their own. If you really want to help your students succeed, you must treat them as whole people. Sometimes you will be called upon to help students in special circumstances. Many students come to your class very distracted by other parts of their lives. You will be much more successful at your central teaching goal if you consider ways to make the learning process pleasant, sensitive, and nurturing as well.

Here are some tips:

1. Make it a point to always present yourself in class smiling and pleasant, creating a positive atmosphere at the very start. Students come to class with all kinds of distracting thoughts that can affect their class experience negatively. Distractions range from the weather to bad news from home. However, if the teacher consistently appears pleasant and cheerful upon entering the room it can be the difference between a good learning experience for your students and another so-so day for them.

2. Focus your attention on the student's attention span. Working on Oral English is a demanding task that requires a great deal of focus. In order to avoid losing your students to their daydreams or worries, I first suggest that you prepare a spectrum of topics and approaches, rather than one long, engaging exercise that will tend to tire their minds. Get them warmed up with a few quick topics such as the weather report, a current event, a piece of campus news, announcements concerning a coming holiday, the next exam day or other events that will grab the students' attention. Change the subject and the material several times through the course of each hour class session. I often bring with me into class an object which helps to focus their attention and gives them a welcome respite from staring at a page or simply listening.

Then after a lively opening, you can go to the readers and do a Read Along story followed by a discussion. Then you might give a Follow Along lecture on China's fixed currency rates. And finally, you might work on pronunciation with *The Word Sheet*. Moving from one subject and method to another keeps the class interesting and extends the student attention span. If we get into a discussion in which they are obviously engrossed and the discussion is active, then we stay on it until we run down. I don't like to interrupt the students when they are truly engaged with their learning. Finally, it's always good to cap off a hot discussion with a good reconcilable conclusion.

As I mentioned before, the weather has a big effect upon classroom attention. In winter everyone stays indoors much of the time, so studying and classroom sessions are more comfortable than the outdoors, but when spring weather hits the campus, the minds of most students begin to wander toward outdoor activities. At this time, social life, shopping, and just taking walks or playing sports all begin to occupy the students' minds again. To bring their wandering attention back to the classroom, you must increase the excitement factor of topics or even activities. In other words, bring on the action and make your class sessions a little more interesting! In teaching language skills we have much more opportunity to do this than, say, a math teacher. How do you make math more "interesting"? But in language labs we have more latitude to choose class topics and vary them to hold the students' attention. We should use that freedom when spring arrives and the warmer weather begins to have its effect on us.

3. Try using object lessons to capture student attention and open up the teaching possibilities. Object lessons are not for small children only. Young adults and adults enjoy learning something new through the eye gate. When I open the class – with a greeting and a smile – I may hold up a gavel brought to class from my office desk, asking the name in English *and* Chinese. Object lessons get everybody's attention and make for good discussion. We can talk about the judicial process; we can talk types of wood and wood finishes; we can talk shapes, and on and on, ad infinitum. So, an object (Try your baby picture!) can provoke a lot of interest and is always good for openers.

4. Make sure to provide one-on-one attention to your students. It is possible and important. I have had classes ranging in number from 30 to 120 and have always managed to offer one-on-one help for each student. Whether you're using Read Along, Talk Along or the Word Drill, in all cases you can engage your students one-on-one by moving around the classroom from one section to another, working with individuals on a word with which they are having trouble. For example, let's take the word *call*. As they are repeating after me, I create different sentences using the word *call*, such as *"Did you call me?" "No, I didn't call you, but I did call Richard, but he didn't hear me when I called his name."* As I move through the class having them repeat the sentences with me, I make eye contact with individual students, stopping by them and leaning over and listening to their pronunciation. You may then ask them to repeat the word or phrase for you, and then you repeat it correctly for them until they get it. After a couple of months with a class, you pretty well know which students need the most help. Using this method of Follow Along combined with one-on-one brings some surprising results. You can use the direct contact one-on-one with any of the speech methods, Read Along, Talk Along, or the Word Drill. Any time you can give this direct contact to the students it assures them that they are getting your personal attention, and you will see their smile of approval.

In a discussion of discipline, I urged you to make direct eye contact with students during class sessions. However, making this personal contact with students will not only help to maintain order, it is also very important to the students personally. We all like feedback and attention when we are trying to improve our skills. The foreign teacher is a special person to most students, and they look to us for an authoritative assist to them in improving their skills. If I can make personal contact with any student, I am helping him in more ways than one. One-on-one is what all students really long for if they are trying to make strides in their English skills. So I make this one-on-one contact in different ways. For example:

A trip to town: When you need an interpreter in town – perhaps you are looking for a special item – why not invite a student to come along with you? This gives the student a chance to have a one-on-one encounter with you, and it's always appreciated. This is especially helpful to your higher comprehenders. Their good language skills can help you, and you can help them improve by pointing out a few mispronunciations and perhaps a couple of new words. I keep the mobile phone numbers of several students that I can call upon.

Chance meetings on campus: Gabbing with the students when you find them on campus or in the shops is another way to make personal contact and give special attention to each individual student. If you see one of your students on campus, take the time to stop a few minutes if you possibly can. They appreciate your going out of your way to talk to them. If they're eager to talk, then give them a little of your time, and it will make their day and give them some English conversation practice.

Of course, you can't expect to go on outings with or stop to talk to every student in your class, but in the classroom you can also achieve one-on-one if you **walk the classroom.** When I am doing a Talk Along, and I have them following me in a lecture, I walk the room. I walk up and down the aisles, moving constantly sometimes slow, sometimes fast. As I wander the aisles, I make eye contact with the students as we continue in Talk Along. I will suddenly stop when they're not pronouncing a particular word correctly and call for a drill. All the while I am listening for wrong pronunciation. When I hear it, I stop and sometimes even bend over students' desks, giving them all of my attention as they repeat the word with me. They usually smile with great delight, glad for the attention. I use this direct contact with the students in all of my teaching activities. It's good when giving a drill because you are able to listen to each student pronounce the word throughout the class. When you hear the word being butchered, stop the drill, move to that student and work with him or her until the pronunciation is correct.

In class, always be looking for any chance to make personal contact or strike up a personal one-on-one conversation. It never fails to lift the spirit of your class.

Another time you can offer a little personal attention is during an oral exam: You can make some helpful comments to students and offer some special advice to them about their speech, and what they must work on to better themselves. They appreciate this, and the oral exam desk becomes an opportunity to speak to the student at close range.

Through the many methods of teaching and the events we share with students in a classroom setting, there are many opportunities to give them some one-on-one attention that adds up to quite a bit of personal attention over a year of classes. Take advantage of every chance you have to make that one-on-one contact, even if it's in a friendly greeting passing each other on campus. The eye contact, a gesture, a smile, or a word or two of comment such as "That's very good." or "Oh, that's better than the first time!" is encouraging to the student.

Speaking of personal contact, I have most of my social contact outside of my apartment because I like privacy and solitude. My apartment becomes my isle of seclusion, and I carefully let my students and my colleagues know this. I make all appointments to talk on or off campus, perhaps in a restaurant for lunch. Other foreign teachers love to have their Chinese friends in their homes anytime, so you can have it either way. I mention this here to let you know that your preferences will be respected and honored in this regard by your friends and students.

Special Attention for Special Students

While we are on the subject of giving individual attention to our students in the learning environment, let me share with you the importance of paying attention to *special* students. Of course, your LC's should also be given this consideration, but there is more than one way to be *special*. Some students may need extra attention because they are under some form of duress. Special students can come from any background, from the poor countryside village, or from an affluent family in a large city. They may hang out on the outer edges of the class. They are sometimes not popular with the in-group or the inner circle of the more popular students.

Then there is another category of student to whom I try to give special attention: the resentful or *I-hate-college* student. There are not many, but I have had a few. Most Chinese families are closely bonded, but sometimes a child may be shunted off to college because the father is in business and the mother is also busy in the business or other activities, and college seems a good place to deposit the daughter or son. As teachers, we must observe our students carefully, and if possible, and if we are willing to spend a little time and maybe the cost of a meal at a nearby restaurant, give some special attention to students who may need some direction in life. Sometimes taking students aside to show your personal interest in their future can impact them for good. We may not succeed every time, but we must try if we find a student in need.

I will never forget one student I had, a young girl who seemed to be depressed. I watched her and gave her special attention in class sometimes, commending her when she did well. It always made her light up. I remember when we were all returning from Spring Festival holiday, and I was approaching the steps of the administration building. There she sat squatting against the wall of the building alone. It looked so unnatural for a girl. She was always quiet and never responsive.

I stopped and said, "Hello, Joanie (not her real name)."

Only her eyes moved to look up at me. When she saw me, she muttered a hello in a very subdued voice. After that day, I tried to cheer her up by directing questions to her in class. I knew she would answer well, and then I could commend her for it. I finally decided I would take her to lunch with me and spend some time with her. I wanted to get her to talk with me and see me as a friend in which she could confide, a grandfather she could talk to. Days turned into weeks, and I kept saying to myself that I would take her to a nice restaurant and encourage her with some special personal attention, but before I knew it the school year was over. Joanie had returned home, and I was off to Switzerland climbing the glaciers in the Alps with my friend, Beat. I thought of her often even then and resolved that when I returned to campus in August that Joanie would be my number one priority. I would give her all of my attention and help her in any way I could. When I returned to campus, Joanie did not return to college. She had committed suicide during the summer, and I never saw her again. I had lost her. To this day I weep at every remembrance of her. She has taught me a great lesson! She made me very mindful of my special students who may need my special attention. Teachers, you never know what some students bring into a classroom hidden away in their hearts. I still see Joanie's face, and I want to see it to remind myself that my kids may be hurting and need me as a friend.

Watch them and love them, especially those who appear depressed, who need your special attention and loving concern. Thanks to Joanie, I don't see any of my students through dry eyes anymore.

An Extreme Suggestion

One semester I had about ten really poor students who were just not going to make it through college with good grades. They paid attention and were good students in class, but seemed to have a mental block that was not allowing them to make the grade. In such cases, you may want to ask the dean of your department if you can hold a special class for these LC students. May I suggest that you make the offer to do this for no pay for you or by the students? I call mine the *Special Students' Class*. I limit the number to the very few who seem to be extremely dyslexic or lacking in motivation. It is said that Einstein and many other great intellectuals were dyslexic. Sometimes a little special attention will carry a special student over the barrier that hinders him. I may ask some high comprehenders to help me in such an afternoon class when they have no classes. They always are happy to do this because it helps them also to assist with these classes. Just one class a week with a small group can make a big difference.

By way of illustration, I had a boy in class one semester that I considered to be hopeless! Everything about his speech was terrible, but his attitude was always so upbeat. He always seemed to maintain a smile. Above all, he clung to his desire to speak English well, and his attention in class was intense. I gave him special attention and asked him to work with me on a couple of class projects. I had him in my classes for two years.

When he graduated, he ranked among my best English-speaking students! He now has an excellent job in Shanghai. This is very rewarding to me as a teacher, and I never resent any of the extra time I spend with these special students.

Chapter Twelve
The English Corner: The Classroom Without Walls

The classroom, well conducted and infused with a positive energy, is a wonderful place for students to work on their English speaking skills. However, it isn't the real world, and sometimes making that transition from classroom to workplace or social setting can trip a student up. As a foreign teacher, you will most likely get the opportunity to occupy a different kind of teaching space called *The English Corner* that is a free space to practice English conversation skills.

The English Corner is a designated meeting place on campus, as a rule outdoors, where usually once a week any and all students are invited to gather to hold dialogues in English. Each campus has its own unique program. Sometimes the Oral English teachers are present and conduct the sessions, but on other campuses the gatherings are in the hands of the students, and teachers sometimes do not attend. If The English Corner is part of your job description, you will find it an ideal place to meet and become acquainted with many English-speaking students who do not attend English classes. It is also an opportunity to meet and collaborate with the other foreign teachers as well.

There are several ways to hold English corner sessions. Here are few basic formats I have found that the students enjoy. You can adopt any variation of these to make English Corner interesting and attractive:

The group discussion session: The teacher(s) in charge divide the students into groups and appoint capable students to lead the others in small group discussions on topics chosen by the group or introduced by the group leader. Subjects could cover some recent news event or a national development, an international sports competition event, or any other topic that is of special interest. Many students appreciate this method because in a smaller group, more students are able to take part and use their English. Indeed, the advantage of the group discussion is that everyone has more opportunity to speak or share an opinion.

The lecture/discussion session: If the foreign teacher in charge has a special subject he wants to treat, then this is a good method. Remember, though, if you decide to lecture to this larger crowd outdoors, you will need to use a loud and clear voice, and if possible, gain a higher footing than the crowd. I happen to have a good strong voice and have no problem with making myself heard, but this may not be a good method for some of the lady teachers or anyone who might have a softer voice. In these sessions you can use an object or give a Follow-Along lecture, pronouncing certain difficult words as you go along. It's also a good idea to mix the lecture session with some new words, articulating pronunciation of certain words and doing a little Talk Along started with, "Follow me." to keep the students participating as you're speaking. Lectures at English Corner work well as long as you can have participation and student involvement. You may want to stop and ask a question. I often call on individual students to dialogue with me on the subject. This always wakes everybody up. Keep the element of surprise alive when you lecture by doing several different things as you move along on your subject, but always remember that

English Corner has as its primary purpose student participation. So keep your students involved and participating, whatever method you use.

The Talk Along session: Talk Along is always fun and helpful to the students. Use it in the lecture session described above to achieve participation or in whatever you plan to talk about with the students. For example, I speak a lot about China's economic development in the present and future and often bring news articles into class dealing with that subject. You can also use news articles effectively with English Corner groups. I sometimes have copies made and hand them out so we all have "a lesson sheet" as we discuss the subject together. Combining Talk-Along with special business news discussions captures interest and facilitates learning English at the same time.

The object lesson session: Everybody likes to look at something you're talking about; it gives the eye something to do while the ear is engaged. This is especially true if the object is unusual or unfamiliar to the students. An object lifted up for everyone to see will grab the crowd's attention. You can use a small object such as a clock or small digital alarm. I have a small talking clock, which I, on one occasion, held up for all to see, and we discussed all the descriptive features of the clock, differentiating between analog and digital clocks. We talked about the features of the clock and the many important reasons we use clocks: for games, to track competition, and for travel schedules. You can go on forever and all the while the students are learning new words about timekeeping. Sometimes you can really have fun with an English Corner group by bringing an object that is a real mystifier. I have several such items in my collection, objects I have collected from my travels over the world in the past fifty years. I have a large fish scale I bought in the Amazon taken from a large Pirarucu fish. I pass it around and have them guess what it is. The discussion gets exciting, and everyone becomes involved. I have used mirrors, pocketknives, and whistles for such object lessons. These object sessions are one of the students' favorite kinds of discussions.

Another version of the object lesson that provokes a lot of interest involves using students as models. I ask one or two students to come and stand near me and then ask the group to start naming the nouns seen on the models. On the face alone there are scores of nouns. This is always fun and always brings some laughter as we describe what we see on the models.

These are a few methods for English Corner, but they are only basic outlines. Your imagination sets the limits for the ways you can evoke conversation and participation in the group who has come out to English Corner. Remember, this is a purely voluntary session, and if you want to have good crowds, keep your English Corner interesting, and above all *give the students an opportunity to speak English.*

Attendance at voluntary English Corners will give you just another piece of evidence of the high level of motivation that Chinese students have for learning the English language. You will want to give them as many resources as you can. I am continually asked by Chinese students, inside and outside of class, *"How can I improve my oral English?"* I have a list that I like to keep on hand on such occasions. This list includes nine additional ways that a student can accomplish his or her goals in English. It is really appreciated by the more motivated students and I reproduce it here for your convenience.

Figure 12.1

Nine Ways Students Can Improve Their English

1. Short wave radio – Simply listen to any channel broadcasting in English. Even the Chinese or Russian stations have very good English speaking announcers. Of course, VOA – Voice of America – and BBC – British Broadcasting Company – have the pure American and British announcers with English teaching programs.

2. English tapes – either commercially prepared or of your classes, if you have a recorder. Record your class sessions (with your teacher's permission) and play them with earphones. Plug in audio English tapes instead of music.

3. English speaking friend – Speak together and learn one new English word every day. Trade words at the end of the day to double your efforts!

4. Discipline yourself to speak only English for 1 or 2 hours at a set time each day – Get several of your classmates to agree to do this with you. Some may laugh at your seriousness, but that's okay. When graduation comes, you'll be getting the better job and a higher exam grade that will carry you to success and the fulfillment of your dreams.

5. Newspapers, magazines, and the Internet – Read aloud to get the full benefit.

6. Get the most out of your classes – Be attentive and take every minute seriously. Stay focused and participate.

7. Attend every extra-curricular English activity that's held on the campus – including English Corner and other student-organized activities.

8. Try reading an English dictionary through – If you have the resolve to improve vocabulary and reading skills, this will pay you big dividends! It's not an impossible task. Don't vow to read it all at once, but to read perhaps three new words each day starting with *A*, then on to *B* and *C*, and so on.

9. When you go on holiday, take an English novel with you – The longer the holiday, the thicker the novel.

As a foreign teacher, you will find that demand for your instruction and assistance is not limited to the classroom. I encourage you to embrace your important role in your new community.

Chapter Thirteen
An Introduction to Grading Oral English

The Peculiar Grading Characteristics of Oral English

An average Entry Comprehension Level Score – ECLS – for a freshman class is going to be about 5.3 to 5.5 of a perfect score of 10. On a grading scale of 100 points, that translates into 53 to 55. That, of course, is a failing grade in the 100 point grading system. Note that this is the *class* average and does not reflect any one student's ECLS. If a class has an average comprehension level (CL) of 5.3, this means the individual scores will range from a low of 4.1 to a high of perhaps 7.0. There is no way to grade an oral student on a perfect 100 point score and have that grade score reflect the true skills of a student in an Oral English class in relation to his or her peers. In a given class you may have a high ECLS of 6.9. This is exceptionally high for a freshman student just out of high school. The low score in that same class may well be a 4.5 or a 4.9, so there is a variation of CL's in any given class between the 40's and 60's. This means that if we gave grades based on the 10-point grade score and then carried them over to the 100-point system, most students would have failing grades!

For this reason there must be a grading system that will correct this imbalance and reflect the grade that is deserved. We call this system the Coefficient Grading System. Teachers have used it for many subjects, but it adapts very well in Oral English grading. Let's look at this problem now in more detail so we are sure to understand how to establish a true grade in Oral English. These principles apply to any Chinese/English class as well.

Grading Oral English is *Another Cup of Tea*

First, we must understand that ECLS's are not grades. They are taken upon entry at the beginning of the school year. The score that determines a student's intellectual achievement is a score taken at exam times through the school semester. It is this grade (and not an entry score) that we are talking about here.

On the 100-point scale, all students scoring below sixty will have a failing grade. And yet, a 5.8 or 5.9 in Oral English for a freshman is equal academically to a grade of between a B and a C. Half or more of some freshman classes will score anywhere from 4.9 to 5.9 on their oral exams. This means they are getting grades in the failing fifties, but realistically these are B students. So we must use a grading system that can give an oral student a realistic grade that reflects a score in the same range of academic achievement as the other subjects he or she is taking. The Coefficient Grading System is the answer for Oral English teachers who want to give accurate individual grades to each student.

It is important to give students grades that are *appropriately* generous, but it is a mistake to give students grades that are *overly* generous. I once took on a class whose previous teacher had given everyone grades between A+ and B- and nothing lower, but when I gave those students their ECLS scores, I found that the grades he had handed out were very generous and inaccurate, not at all reflecting the actual skill of each student. If you want to pass a student on the edge of failure, there is a way to do that using the coefficient system, but it is this teacher's opinion that it is only fair to the student to give each student a grade that reflects his or her actual academic level as it relates to students taking the same course. It is not fair to students when they have no idea of their actual level of achievement because their grades have been given to them gratuitously. Grading a student properly is certainly one of the things students pay for when they enter the college program. Accurate grading gives the teacher a chance to counsel students who need improvement and encourage them to study harder, and a less than desirable grade will motivate ambitious and intent students to try harder. For students who work hard and actually achieve high marks, those grades truly mean something when the grades are distributed honestly. In other words, accurate grading should be a matter of priority to teachers.

A good way of scoring the Oral English student, especially if you use oral exams as your exam method, is the dividing of the grade of each student between his class performance and his academic exam scores. Doing this, we will have a grade that can be translated easily into a letter grade that actually reflects the true achievement of the student. The coefficient grading system allows us to give an accurate grade that parallels the 100 point score that we find on a written exam.

The Coefficient Method of Grading

This system is simple, but involves a little more work at the end of the term when making up the final grades. I use it because it is simply the most realistic scoring method for Oral English grading.

Simply put, the grade is divided between a class behavior grade and the academic performance grade (the average of oral exams scores) for the term:

- **The class performance grade** of 100 will be 30% of the total term grade.

- **Academic scores** totaling 70% of the total term score are taken from exam scores. Exam scores can reflect written or oral examination. I use at least two oral exams only.

The Class Performance Grade

You will multiply 0.3 x 100 (30%) which equals 30. The perfect grade is 100. I usually start all students at 96. If they perform exceptionally well in class, I give them 100. Their score will be 30. If they perform badly in class, e.g., talking, distracting, clowning, needing continual correcting, being continually late or frequently absent without excuse, cheating, and so forth, then the score will go down with each infraction which I record in the folder that holds my class roster. In such instances I write the students' names and briefly describe the misdemeanors on slips of paper. I throw the papers into the folders and then pull all of them out at the end of the term during grading to determine if their behavior merits being graded down.

In such cases, instead of the full 30 points students should make at the end of each semester, they may receive class behavior/participation grades of only 15 or 20. This will take their final grades down considerably. I have only had two students I had to punish by reducing their class participation grade. They were friends and as usual, the one was a very bad influence on the other boy, and they continually needed correction in class. They were also absent from class frequently (together) and also left class together during class breaks. They were both quite good comprehenders, but their class behavior brought their grade down, nearly causing one of the boys to fail the class.

Excellence in class performance and participation will merit the full 100, but this is rare. I may have two or three such students in a class of thirty. The perfect coefficient grade of 100 is 30. If the student who performs exceptionally in class has a low exam grade, this high class participation grade can help him raise his total grade.

Now turn to the exams. Add all exam grades together (at least two or more), and then divide by the number of exams to get your average grade for that student. You then multiply that average of all exam grades by 0.7. This gives you the academic grade of that student.

To get the final grade, you add the 0.7 figure of all exams (academic) score to the 0.3 class participation score, and you will have a realistic grade for that student which will reflect his actual total class performance. See grading examples in *Figure 13.1*.

Figure 13.1

Grading Examples

Class Performance	Class Exam Scores	Final Grade
28.8[1]	66.4[2]	95.2[3]

[1] 0.3 of his performance grade of 96
[2] 0.7 x the average of his 2 oral scores at the exam
[3] This is a good score.

This gives the student an A grade and reflects his true grade as a good student in class with high comprehension scores.

Say you have a slightly above average student with a 5.6 academic grade. His semester grade would be:

Class Performance	Class Exam Scores	Final Grade
28.8[1]	56.4[2]	84.6[3]

[1] (0.3 x 96) A good student applying himself in class.
[2] 0.7 x the average of his total exam grades
[3] This gives him a B grade and reflects his true level of achievement.

If a student with low exam grades also has a dismal class performance, it will bring his final grade down noticeably. This is as it should be. He may be a good comprehender and a poor student! In that case his performance grade reflects his weakness in class performance.

Another good thing about the coefficient grading system is that if you explain this grading method to the students when classes begin, they realize that their class performance is a part of their final grade, and it tends to motivate them to do a little more in class. But the best thing about this system is that it combines performance and behavior with academics to give us a realistic score for every student, good or bad.

A teacher must concentrate carefully when scoring and evaluate each skill carefully on its own merit. It is important not to rely upon your knowledge of that student's previous performances or his or her background. *In fact, I make it a point NOT to look at the student's previous scores until after I have given the exam.* I want to see how he or she compares only *after* I have graded the present performance.

Another thing to keep in mind when it comes to fairness in grading is that it's better to give a speech skill grade on a variety of skills you choose, rather than on just one skill such as pronunciation, the reason being that many fine students with a high skill in pronunciation may have a low vocabulary. The result will be a score that fails to reflect the full spectrum of a student's speech skills. I have come to realize from experience that a speech score should reflect several or all of a student's skills. I place a lot of emphasis on pronunciation, but I have had excellent students who were extremely conversant and had mastered their second language skills well, even though they had much to be desired in pronunciation. If I had scored them only on their pronunciation, it would have dragged their semester grade down and produced an unfair grade.

Exams are a very important part of the learning process, but scoring Oral English students can be difficult if we want to give the student a grade that reflects his or her actual skill at different stages in the learning process. So that you will know what to expect, I will give you a sense of the comprehension scores you can expect at different stages in a student's education. Most students coming into the first year of college will have a comprehension level between the upper 40's to perhaps a 6.0. The average freshman class level will be between 5.2 and 5.4. This means the lower scores (a few) will be in the 40's. There will be a few in the upper 50's. Most of the students will grade in the 50's. Each year the students' levels will increase until many of them, the better students, will be scoring in the mid and upper 60's, with a few achieving a 7.0 or higher.

Comprehension scores are rigid. That is, whether you are a freshman or a senior with a high or low comprehension, everyone is graded or scored within the same range of scoring, between 4.0 and 9.0. Does this mean everyone in the 50's gets a D grade while those scoring in the 60's get a B? That is, the lower the comprehension, the lower the grade? No, of course not. Students must be graded by the skills they show at their level of education.

To grade a student in oral skills properly, I have found it important to create a class curve using the class average of each class as the mid-grade. For example, say you have 30 students in your freshman class. Upon entry you give them each an ECLS. Now add all the scores together and divide by the number of students. This gives you your average CL for that class. Let us say the average score of that class is 5.3. You then make that 5.3 the average grade, which is a C. Those with the lower scores grade downward from there. Those with higher scores grade upward from there.

In a good senior English major class your average may be a whopping 6.6! This means that many of your students have speech skills scoring in the 70's (7.0) and higher. That 6.6 would be your C grade, even though it is much higher than the average in your freshman class. The grades would be comparable, reflecting the true skills of that class. You may then arbitrarily set the grade scores on the down side and the up side from the 6.6. The student with the 6.6 has very good comprehension, but there are students in that class who have much higher total speech skills *along with* comprehension, such as having an excellent vocabulary and pronunciation. So, no matter what the score level may be, you have a true and realistic scoring all within the range of 4.0 and 9.0 for that class and its particular level of skill.

Determining the Class Grade Cluster

Right now I have a student with a 7.7 in a class averaging 5.6. In this case, this student gets the A+ and then I exclude her score from the average, so my class average score will not be distorted by her extraordinary speech skill score.

In another class I have a boy who understands nothing. His comprehension is zilch! He will get a failing grade, and I will exclude his score from the cluster of scores of the other students.

Scores that are removed from the cluster of grades by one whole comprehension level of 10 points (1.0) distort the average and must not be included in the grade cluster. I removed both of these students from the average score of the class lest they distort the average score and move the C grade from true center of the actual class average. In other words, extreme fringers either to the far high comprehension or the extreme low comprehension must not be figured into the average. In this process, the extreme high and low students receive their rightful grades, but the class average is kept stable, reflecting the true average. The grades should be clustered together, and in most cases they are, but sometimes you do have a student or two on the extreme outskirts, for better or worse!

Chapter Fourteen
Exam Basics

As I have demonstrated, the objective of every Oral English teacher should be to improve the English speaking skills of their students by using his or her own native English language effectively in the classroom. Competent and professional Chinese English teachers provide the Chinese student with everything but that native speech that is natural to the foreign English teacher. As foreign teachers, we should keep our responsibilities clearly in mind when we come to China to teach. Our first objective should be to actually improve the English speech skills of our students, and we must continually work to improve our teaching methods so that they produce the desired results for our students. I would also like to impress upon you that we have an obligation to the *parents* of our students. These parents work long and hard over the years to scrape together enough money to send their children to college so they will have a better life through education. Some students come from the countryside from homes where the parents work and sweat through the heat of the day, doing without many necessities to put aside every yuan for their children's education. When these students come into my classroom, I want to be sure the parents get their money's worth.

Taking exams seriously is an important part of the foreign teacher's responsibility. Exams, which are administered two to three times each semester, serve many purposes. They not only indicate the progress of the student in acquiring skills in spoken English, but they also serve to indicate to the teacher if the methods being used in the classroom are actually working. Exams measure the progress of the student over a semester or a term.

Here are the major types of exams that can be administered in Oral English:

I. The Entry Comprehensive Level Score – ECLS – exam is an oral exam given to each student at the beginning of a new class term. Remember, this is a score and is not a grade. It only serves to let the teacher know the English skill level of each student upon entry. This data helps the teacher to tailor teaching approaches to meet the needs of each student and also to plan larger class strategies by learning which students are high comprehenders and which are low, as well as the average comprehension level – CL – of the entire class.

II. The Graded Comprehensive Level Score exam – GCLS – is the same as the ECLS except it is given as a graded exam later in the semester.

Both of these exams involve an oral interview with the teacher. The basic difference between these two exam forms is simply that one is given as a score at the beginning of the term only to determine comprehension for the teacher's information, while the other is a score given later in the semester that becomes part of the grade the student earns that semester.

III. Written Exams – While the Oral English course grade should be based primarily upon oral exams, there are instances in which a written exam is appropriate. On occasion, I will conduct a written exam if I find the content matter in a lecture or reading to be especially apt or important, for example.

Conducting a written exam requires a fair amount of preparation. Seating conditions in some classrooms are often quite close quarters and not at all good exam conditions. It's easy for students to look over on another student's paper, so I have a set of strict rules for exam time and take ample time before each exam to explain my rules and my strict discipline policy if I catch someone cheating.

Here are the rules under which I run a test, which my students have become very familiar with when we have a written exam:

1. All books, dictionaries and papers are to be removed from the top of your desk.

2. Write your name, the date and class name from left to right across the top of the paper in that order, and turn your paper over with the writing down.

3. Cover your paper with your other hand when you're writing.

4. When you finish writing an answer, turn your paper over with the backside up and the writing down. An exposed paper creates an uncomfortable temptation to those sitting on either side of you.

5. When you have finished writing on your paper, turn it over and wait for further instruction.

6. Lay your pencils down when you're finished.

7. Keep papers turned down until instructed to turn them up again.

8. When all pencils or pens are laid down on the desk, we exchange papers when the teacher indicates. I then instruct the students how to score the papers.

9. Then the student who graded the paper must write his English name on the bottom back of the paper that he graded.

10. Do not grade your own paper.

11. Turn the papers up and never, never touch the original answer with your pen or pencil! Put no marks on the papers except the grade as you are instructed.

12. Write the score in large numbers in the center of the paper with a circle around it.

IV. Written Mini-Exam – These are class lecture exams, or mini exams. I give them one quarter-sized sheet of paper. Each student is required to write his or her name on the left top of the paper, the date in the middle, and the class number on the right. After giving the exam questions, usually five or ten questions, we exchange the papers and the students quickly grade the papers, which I check over again later. The name of the grading student is again – always – written at the bottom backside of the test paper as we have mentioned above. I critique the papers, pointing out how instructions were and were not followed on the paper by the student and the grader. This follow-through, evaluating how instructions were carried out, helps students to develop a keener sense of the importance of carefully following instructions, which I continually point out to them as being essential when they start working in the real world after graduation.

I will often announce mini-exams for the next class that will cover the material we covered in today's class session. That means that anything and everything I'll be teaching today could be in the exam next class. I especially like to have students memorize simple outlines on a given subject such as the Five Elements of Information, i.e., *who, what, why, where,* and *when.* In my Business English class (business management, basic enterprise economics), I may be treating gross and net profits and ask for five overhead items that have to be paid from monthly gross income. I ask them to list five items, one through five. It's a simple exam but accomplishes its purpose, especially when you give two or more such exams each month. It keeps the students on their toes and encourages taking notes and listening carefully.

When giving a written exam, you should have a different exam for each class, if possible. Chinese young people often feel that to help their friends to know what the test was about is a matter of friendship and being helpful, having nothing to do with giving the students in later classes an unfair advantage.

Paying attention to something as simple as how you gather the exam papers at the end of a written exam can prove to be quite a revelation and help to the teacher. The order in which exam papers arrive provides information that helps me to more fully understand my students. I am careful to put the first exam paper handed to me on the top as I gather them from the students leaving the room. This way when the last student has handed in his or her paper, I have the exam paper of the first student on top and the last exam paper to be handed me on the bottom, in that order. Then when all the papers are in my hands, I number them in the corner from 1 through 28. Then I forget the order of the exams as they were handed in until I finish grading the papers. I put the highest graded paper on top and the lowest scores on the bottom. Then I go through them and compare the location of that score with the number that indicates how soon they finished their exam. When I finish grading the papers, I have data that will help me to conduct a very interesting analysis of my students that will help me to better understand their learning habits.

For example, here is Steve, an excellent student but, alas, his was one of the last to be handed to me along with Anthony, one of my struggling special – LC – students. The first three papers were handed to me by three of my top students and, true to form, they made the three highest scores along with Steve who handed in his paper next to last!

This detail tells me that Steve may have some learning problems and that he labored over his paper two or three times to make sure of his answers. The first three finished quickly and didn't work nearly as hard as Steve, but they all made the first five high scores. This tells me a lot about Steve. It tells me he is working hard to stay up at the head of the class with the others. It is important to pay attention to the smallest of details if you really want to get to know your students. I notice, for example, that my three top students were smiling when they handed in their paper, but Steve was frowning under the strain of effort. This lets me know that I must give Steve a good deal of encouragement and express an appreciation for his efforts. Otherwise, he may get discouraged and his performance may suffer. My smiling, quick-to-the-finish students might need a little extra challenge. Indeed the order in which students turn in their exams can be very telling. For example, in any one class, my struggling students will tend to finish their exams at different times. I have four failing grades when I score the papers, but when I look at the number up in the corner of the paper I see that two of them handed their exam papers in early, and two of them stayed till the last to hand their exams. I conclude that those students who hand in their papers too quickly were not trying as hard as the two who waited and pored over their exam paper again and again. This tells me that the culprit was, in part, bad study habits for the students who finished hurriedly. A good Talk Along lecture on that subject was needed. Another thing I look at when I grade exam papers is how many times a student has changed answers on his exam sheet. This indicates a certain measure of struggle, but also effort.

When you score your exams, you will notice that your best students are your best participators. Not all participators score high on exams, but your best students will develop their skills through their enthusiastic involvement in class activities. Pointing this correlation out to your students can motivate them to get more involved.

If I have a class that's hard to manage, I give more written exams than I give to my good classes. First, it keeps students more attentive when they know they're going to be tested in the next class. Secondly, in a class that's difficult to manage you will have lower grades. More exams give those students more opportunity to bring their grades up and may make the difference between passing and failing.

Chapter Fifteen
The Oral Exam

Oral English teaches the practical use of all oral speech skills. As teachers of this particular phase of the students' English language course, it only stands to reason that oral exams should be the primary method of testing their speech skills. An Oral English teacher must develop skill in the administration of oral exams. Written exams can be used in Oral English for testing the students' ability to retain useful information or to judge the students' level of class participation or note taking on subject material given in class, but the oral exam is vital to testing the students' oral skills. If you are learning to fly an airplane, you will be tested by actually flying that airplane by yourself on a solo flight. If you are learning to be a carpenter, the test of your skill is when you can build a house yourself. When you are learning to speak English, the proof of your skill is in performing your English speech skills. It's the same principle we apply to testing the speech skills of a student by giving the oral exam.

The Comprehension Exam

Comprehension involves the dual abilities of being able to understand *and* speak with another English-speaking person. The English speech skill is not the ability to write and memorize a speech, and then present it before others. There is very little comprehension involved in this kind of language performance. The word *comprehension* implies communication in which two or more people are exchanging ideas and conversing on a given subject. In a speech competition, there is very little or no conversation involved, even though such a competition can be an excellent method to develop other important language skills such as composition and public speaking.

When I use the word *comprehension*, I use it in its true meaning referring to the ability of a student to understand *and be understood* in English. To develop the student's speech skills, the Comprehension Level Score – CLS – should be used frequently in grading.

My advice for new teachers to China is to begin every class semester with an Entry Comprehension Level Score – ECLS. This is for your experience as a new teacher and for the students' sake as it helps them to receive the help they will need in class. Remember, this score is not a grade and so accuracy is not crucial, but at the same time you will learn accuracy by administering the ECLS. Remember, the ECLS' results will help you to determine how to organize your class and strategize your term. The ECLS will help you with your seating chart; it will help you to appoint class monitors and secretaries, and it will give you a sense of who needs more help and who would benefit from more of a challenge. Of course, the ECLS is also a benchmark that will help you track the progress of your students over the semester. Each time I give an oral exam I can see any progress from that first CLS score to the present. I have seen students go from 5.3 to 6.8 in three years! The only way to watch a student's progress is to know what his comprehension level was the day he entered your class. Then you have something to compare every oral exam with to know if a student is advancing in his English skills.

Time is of the essence in giving an entry score. Therefore, it's much more expeditious to give a single score for each performance by each student. Remember, you can change this ECLS score if in the course of the school year you hold conversation with a student whose comprehension skills are higher than you scored them in the brief entry interview when he or she was new and nervous. It is important to finish the ECLS quickly so we can get on with classes and get the students involved in their first classes' studies. You will find that the ECLS is welcomed by the students because it will give most of them the chance to talk with a foreign English-speaking person for the first time, and this is a big thrill, especially for freshman students! Some of us who have experience scoring can give an accurate comprehension entry score in a very short time. The trick is to get the student to talk at that early stage in the semester.

You will refer to the CLS score numerous times throughout the school year for help and student information. I often look at this score when a student's answer is exceptionally good to see where I scored him, or when I need an interpreter to go to town with me. You will be surprised how many times and in how many ways through the year this score comes in handy.

Conducting the CLS Exam

The actual CLS exam is conducted using a scoring sheet with five elements of speech listed on it. These will be your grading criteria. You may want to improve the list or change it to your liking. (We will discuss these five elements in depth in a later chapter.) You can grade all of your students on the same sheet with the five elements of speech being scored at the top, or you can use individual score slips with the grading indicators for each skill on each slip. I find it easier to use the slips, so you can quickly score the speech qualities without confusion between students and columns. It takes a little more preparation, but in the end it is easier to score each student and then you have all five scores with a total for the student's reference.

You can usually grade a student in between two to three minutes. You must have concentration and enough time to hear the student if you are to get the most accurate score. The CLS exam need not be intimidating or unpleasant for the student. The topics of conversation can be light and interesting. For example, you can take oral exams after a holiday and ask each student, "*What was the most interesting thing that happened to you on your* holiday?" Or, you can show pictures at a designated exam desk and have individual students come to the exam desk and take the exam sitting across from you. Ask them to explain what they see in the picture. Each student should be asked about the same picture, usually a simple setting, to ensure that each student is presented with the same level of challenge. This maintains fairness. If you decide to change pictures for variety, then you would not want to show a simple one to part of the students and a very complicated picture to others taking the same exam.

There are several different basic settings you can use for oral exams:

1. Set up an exam desk in the front of the room and, with the help of the class monitor, interview each student at the exam desk with you.

2. Give a brief oral exam by calling each student separately outside of the classroom door and interviewing him or her briefly. This method is not the best, but for holding an oral exam to test students' conversational skills, it is acceptable. I have also used this method for the ECLS.

3. Have an *open oral*, calling on each student to stand at his or her seat and give a report on a holiday or some other subject. However, this method has a downside. When students hear each other's reports, you have to observe carefully to make sure they aren't simply parroting one another. They must be given a question that forces them to be original and have their own extemporaneous experience to tell. It is very important that exam answers are kept extemporaneous and that there is no rehearsal or copying involved.

There are several ways I keep the student from parroting other students' answers when giving an open oral exam. Chinese young people are very friendship-oriented, and they may sometimes not feel there is anything wrong with helping "a friend" with the answers during an exam. I do several things to avoid this problem.

First, I have a very effective lecture I give prior to an exam that explains why honesty in an exam is essential. This lecture is one of the many things I am not including in this little manual, but I will point out a couple of things briefly to help you develop your own pre-exam lecture. I tell the story of a boy who copied answers from a girl next to him, but her answers were wrong! I also tell students that taking an exam is not only a test of the knowledge we want you to retain, but also a test of your character. They take moral instruction seriously, and it does help.

Secondly, I keep my oral questions individual. That is, I ask students a question that requires an original answer of their own. For example, I like to give these exams after they return from a holiday. If I simply ask them what they did during their holiday, 80 percent of their answers will be the same. They will parrot what others have said before them. There is a way to get around this: Ask them a more specific question that forces them to be original.

Ask, *"What was the most exciting thing that happened to you while you were on your holidays?"* The answer must be original in this case. Other questions that encourage originality include: *"Tell me about a new friend you met during your holidays." "What was the funniest thing that happened to you on your holidays?" "What was the most interesting thing that happened to you during your holidays?" "Describe for me a day in your father's work."*

These oral report exams are usually given right after they have returned to school from a holiday, at the end of a semester, or long after they are adjusted and comfortable giving such a report before the class. This is a report they will stand and orate extemporaneously (without preparation) to the rest of the class. The teacher will be grading the speech skills of each report.

For the sake of the first few who begin the exam, I usually give them five minutes to think about what they will say before we begin the exam, or ask if three students would volunteer to be the first ones to give their report. When the answer has to be original, I don't care if they talk and discuss it with each other with these specific, individualized questions. They may also discuss the questions with each other in an open classroom in Chinese. It doesn't matter because they will each have to come up with their own experiences in the end. *However, no pens, paper or visible notes should be on their desk during the exam time!* If you take at least three extemporaneous orals each term, including the final, you will have a good picture of that student's true CL by the end of the term.

The things students come up with when they have to be original range from the hilarious to the ingenious. The stories are surprisingly good! One boy told how he stood by a pay phone and let a man use his pre-paid phone card and then the man paid him for using it. By this method, he earned the three yuan he needed to buy his bus ticket! If you succeed at eliminating the tendency to parrot their classmates, you will hear some really interesting stories that will bring tears and laughter. The purely extemporaneous answer gives you a good chance to give that student a true oral grade. In these report exams the low comprehenders often get better scores simply because they have something very interesting or exciting to tell, and they are passionate about what they're saying. One girl at a private desk exam told me how she loved a certain boy very much in her hometown. When she returned home, she met him, and he suddenly opened a small box with an engagement ring in it! Her heart leaped out of her chest! She became speechless. Then he told her how much he loved another girl and needed her to help him present the ring to her. On and on the wonderful stories go ... if you can avoid the parroting.

The oral report of personal experience is a good method of assessing speech skills. These are often fun and entertaining and can be conducted in a group setting. However, an oral exchange between the student and teacher at a designated exam desk has its advantages. In such a setting the student might be less self conscious and able to concentrate, and more of a dialogue between the student and teacher is possible, resulting in a truer measure of *conversation* skills. At the exam desk the teacher might conduct an interview and ask questions, present a picture for the student to explain, have the student read prepared printed materials to test the student's pronunciation and oral reading skills, especially with targeted new or difficult words, or any other method that fosters a verbal exchange between student and teacher.

In the oral report, I will grade the student for his ability to speak extemporaneously with good content and good choice of words. He does not have to have a big vocabulary to get a good score for this exam. He must be able to use his English to describe a real life experience, and if possible, make me laugh or cry (tongue in cheek)! I want him to stay fluent and make me understand.

In an interview exam, I am testing that student's ability to have an oral exchange with me. Can she listen to and understand me as well as she can speak to me? That is, I want to determine two things: how well she understands me, and how well I understand her. A conversation requires the student's ability to speak intelligibly and to hear and understand me correctly. Comprehension is a two-way street. It's not just the student's ability to speak English, but also the ability to converse intelligibly with another English-speaking person. I want my students to become conversant in English. We might call this the ultimate skill. If I take a student to the restaurant to interpret for me, and I order a fresh sliced tomato, I don't mean a fresh sliced potato!

Picture exams: You can carry out a picture exam either with or without an interview format, that is, an exchange between the student and the teacher as we have explained above. In an *interview* exam with pictures I coax the students along to bring more out of them about what they see in a picture. A simple picture provides a very good way to test speech skills. I use the Oxford University materials and in that package there are many colorful illustrations depicting the different topics in the course. I use those pictures, but any photo or illustration that depicts daily life of people is good to use. For example, one illustration I use is of an American kitchen, and the father and his son are preparing food on the table. The picture is "busy" with a lot of things going on. I ask students to look at the picture and tell me what they see, to describe everything they can about that picture. This is a very expeditious way to give an oral exam to test the student's abilities in descriptive language because the material is right before them and they don't have to add a mental recall to the list of skills they are trying to juggle. I use several pictures, so once again, they each must be original and extemporaneous when they start describing what they see in the picture. With the picture method, you are getting a true impression of students' actual ability to describe something in English. Sometimes I ask them to weave a story into the objects or people they see in the picture.

Here are two examples of actual picture exams I gave to one class:

Teacher: *Here is a nice colored picture. What is in this picture?*

Student: A street.

Teacher: *Yes, that's right! Can you tell me more about this street?*

The student hesitates. (Maybe my question wasn't understood clearly).

Teacher: *Is this a city street or a country road? Tell me about this street.*

Student: Oh, it is a city.

Teacher: *And what do you see on this street?*

Student: I see cars and a bicycle, and people walking across the street.

Teacher: *That's good! What are these shops along the street? What kind of shops do you see?*

Student: There are many shops. There is a shop with animals ...

In a conversation interview with a picture you can deduce many qualities from the student's speech. You will have a more precise grade because you will be able to compare who was more fully able to address the details of the picture right there before you, but it takes a little longer and is more practical in classes of thirty or less. Notice that this interview was strained because this student was a low comprehender, and I had to pump the answers out of him to get him to talk, but I also got a good chance to perceive his conversant skills. He did quite well even though I had to pump him.

When introduced to the same picture, another student said, "Oh, there is a mother buying candy for her little boy!"

That is the kind of response that tells me this student has a good command of his English and can more easily express what he sees.

You never know what to expect in these picture exams. For example, at the same picture exam, with the picture of the street scene, a boy who was a low comprehender approached the exam desk. I showed him the picture.

He started out by saying, "Well, Mr. Bill, I went shopping on this street. I want to buy shoes, but the shoes are too much money! So I . . ."

He went on and on with this novel first person shopping spree that shocked the daylights out of me! I didn't know the boy had it in him. Needless to say, he made a very good score on that exam, higher than some high comprehenders! He had this yarn on the tip of his tongue as soon as he saw the picture. I didn't have to pump anything out of him. In fact, I had to stop him long before his story was finished. You'll have many of these surprises working with the students. That's why each student's speech qualities must be judged independently on their own merits at the time of the exam. In a previous exam that same student didn't do very well. So there would be two different grades from two different exams from the same student, with each exam graded on each exam's performance.

When students finish an oral exam, they are not allowed to return to their seats or talk to anyone in the room. They must bring their books with them to the exam table and pass directly from the exam room to a designated classroom until everyone has finished the exam. This way they cannot "help" each other by passing information about the exam to their friends.

In a picture interview exam, I will learn that student's level of comprehension, her ability to understand me, as well as her ability to articulate an answer to me intelligibly, that is, to determine that her answer is a direct response to my question. I will know her vocabulary level as she describes what she sees. In a picture interview exam you can accurately evaluate all five of the speech skills (See Chapter 16) usually used in English speech competitions. The pictures must contain easily identified objects and activities. We're not testing their knowledge of chemistry, but of common objects with which they are familiar and can easily identify.

You can also hold a picture exam without an interview. In this format, the student must fly solo, describing on his or her own the picture or weaving a story into the picture. In such a case the student must speak for at least two minutes without any questions or interruptions from the teacher.

It's very important for fairness' sake to explain to the students the way an exam is going to be carried out before the exam begins. If we fail to make every student understand, then we could be faulted for a student not getting a better grade. Classroom rules numbers 1 and 2 stipulate that they *carefully* listen to instruction and then *carefully* follow the instruction given. So we as teachers must be very sure when giving instructions that everyone understands the instructions and the procedures of an exam before it starts. I use the slogan, *"Let's help each other,"* to signal that they are free to chat in Chinese, allowing them to talk with each other and get the help they need from those around them. I sometimes move through the class and ask several students if they understand everything, or ask for hands if they do not understand. Chinese students take their exams very seriously, and I want to help them do as well as they can.

The pronunciation exam is another option for the exam desk. This is usually a list of words or a paragraph containing words the class has been working on, such as the words located on *The Word Sheet* described earlier. These are words that we have taken from our Read Along sessions during the year of reading together. I give oral pronunciation exams on some or all of these words, or I compose a paragraph that includes words taken from this list. They will each be asked to read the paragraph, and I grade their level of pronunciation. You will want to design your own grading system for pronunciation and create score sheets on your word processor, or buy a form sheet in a local stationer's shop near your campus. There are many forms available that could be used. The good thing about the pronunciation exam is that students cannot help each other during the exam. Each student has only himself to depend upon for good results. The thing we must be careful about in a pronunciation exam is the grading level (score) used. Pronunciation will always bring a low score and can have a bad effect on the total semester grade that may be otherwise quite good. To avoid the negative effect of a pronunciation exam, it's better to avoid scoring on that only. Have more than just pronunciation on one exam. For example, include the words in a paragraph and include a score for reading and articulation – how well the student handled the narration including voice inflection and proper expression – as well as pronunciation. Pronunciation is the weakest skill in most Chinese students and the most difficult to overcome. Vocabulary is a mental skill, but pronunciation is a speech skill that involves very much the physical ability to form the words you have in your vocabulary. To grade a student only on any one particular skill of the five listed on our oral exam sheet is not really fair to the student and especially to the freshmen who may be in their first class ever with a foreign teacher speaking pure native English. If I give an exam on pronunciation only, I will come up with some very low scores for otherwise very good students. Pronunciation is also perhaps the most important of the English skills. I have students with excellent vocabularies, but I can't understand them because their pronunciation is terrible!

When I give a pronunciation exam, I include words with which we are familiar and have covered thoroughly in class. If students have applied themselves to practicing their pronunciation, then they should be ready for the exam. Prior to an exam, I work hard with the students on a list of words I explain to them will be included in the exam. If we work on fifty words, perhaps twenty of them will be in the exam. Exam time is the best time to get the students focused because they become intent when they know they're studying exam materials, but on a pronunciation exam I must include the other skills besides pronunciation. I tell them it is a pronunciation exam to make them work on their pronunciation, and then also score them on other skills such as fluency and expression.

Remember to concentrate attention on the most difficult words in oral English pronunciation. The students can pronounce quite well most of the words they have added to their vocabulary. What we want to do is isolate the ones that are hard to pronounce and work on these in particular. By correcting the hardest to pronounce, we will improve pronunciation across the whole spectrum of their English vocabulary having the same difficult sound.

During each oral exam I make a list of those words I notice which presented the most problems for the student. That list of words then becomes the word list I will concentrate on with that class until I see real evidence of improvement. There are usually between 12 and 20 words on that list. This tells me exactly where we need to focus our attention in our reading and class sessions.

Chapter Sixteen
Administering the Oral Exam

The first score sheet to which I was introduced when I first began to teach in China was for a speech competition. It contained five elements of speech upon which each contestant was to be evaluated. I have modified that original list of five speech skills over the years in an attempt to capture the true qualities of good language skills. I suppose teachers who place as much importance on the oral exam as I do are free to include skills on their CL sheet or oral exam sheets that they feel are appropriate skills. But it's best not to try to have more than five skills to grade lest you become bogged down trying to grade so many items and lose accuracy in the process. It's better to keep it at five and do a more accurate score on the five.

The comprehension score sheet for a memorized speech competition is going to necessarily be different from a comprehension score sheet when giving an oral exam in which the student is called on to speak extemporaneously to his or her teacher at an exam table. In a speech competition, memorization, composition, and pronunciation are the primary factors. In oral exam scoring, on the other hand, we are testing that student's extemporaneous and conversational speech skills which reveal actual comprehension. There is no composition or memorization for an oral exam.

Also, students taking an exam do not have the luxury of time that contestants have in a speech competition. In a speech competition, the judges have perhaps five to ten minutes to judge the five skills of each student, but in an oral exam you are holding a brief dialogue with the student and therefore you don't have the same amount of time. And, you don't really need it. Other experienced foreign teachers will have different criteria for giving a speech exam, and you may want to consult other teachers and then establish your own scoring system, but here we will consider what the norm is among most experienced foreign experts.

A comprehension exam sheet should have a total of ten points as a perfect score. The speech qualities on which you grade a student may vary. My oral score sheet includes the following five qualities of speech:

1. Originality: 1 point
2. Pronunciation: 3 points
3. Articulation: 3 points
4. Conversancy: 2 points
6. Expression: 1 point

The first question some will ask after reading my list of skills will be, *"Pray tell, what is the difference between pronunciation and articulation?"* There's really a lot of difference. Articulation is the student's overall ability to express herself to me, that is, how well she handled her descriptive speech skills. Pronunciation deals with the handling of individual words and sounds. So I make a distinction between articulation and pronunciation. These skills can be used on a comprehension exam sheet and in a speech competition as well as an oral exam standard in the classroom. However, in a speech competition the conversancy (4) would not be scored until after the speech is given, and the judges usually ask the contestants several questions to defend their speech. Once the judges finish questioning the contestant, then they will grade the student on conversancy.

It would surely prove helpful to teachers who have been asked to judge in a speech contest to meet with the other judges and go over the five skills on the score sheet so that all the skills are understood thoroughly. When a teacher saw my list of five skills that I had brought to the competition with my other papers, she asked me the difference between articulation and pronunciation. We were both judges in a speech competition, but she didn't know that difference between those two words, and there is a big difference! A brief meeting of the judges even just prior to the event would ensure a consistent scoring pattern being used by all of the judges and result in each student getting a fairer score.

Let me delve more deeply into each of the five skills that I use to judge oral exams:

1. Originality: This is the quality of the original content the student comes up with. Is it a humdrum approach on an ordinary subject or something interesting or original? Does his subject grab me? Originality reflects how the student chooses to approach his subject. Note this skill is only worth 1 point. Most students will get a .04 score from me. But when that student responds with something outstanding I may score him with a .09 or a whopping 1! If she starts by saying, "*I fell in love with a boy when I was in middle school but my parents disapproved.*" or, "*My trip home was exciting! They caught a thief on the train I went home on last week,*" she has me on the edge of my seat and will most likely score a 1 for originality.

2. Pronunciation: This is the big element in speech quality. It is worth 3 points denoting its importance among the five speech skills. Good pronunciation may get a high rating of 1.9 or a 2.2 for a student with above average pronunciation skill. A poor score would be a 0.9 to 1.2. In teaching Oral English, this is the one skill on which we should especially concentrate and focus in class sessions. It's the skill in which most Chinese teachers are going to be weak, and the chief skill foreigners are called from abroad to perfect. If we are to give the Chinese students something, this is the one thing we are to give them – good pronunciation!

3. Articulation: This rates in importance with me next to pronunciation, as evidenced by its being worth 3 points. Articulation includes several very important qualities of English speech skills. It implies the ability to express oneself well by a good choice of words and structuring your sentences so they convey good clear meaning to the hearers. Pronunciation is the right formation of the sound of a word, while articulation is the right combination of words that best express your meaning. Articulation embraces all the good qualities of speech beyond vocabulary. Oral English is not actually an English class; it is a speech class.

You will note that grammar is a component of articulation. Grammar is not a subject on which we grade heavily in Oral English (as seen in the fact that it is not one of the five elements of skills being scored), but our students are learning grammar in their Chinese English classes, and what they are learning in any English class should be reflected in their English usage in our Oral English class. It's one of those instances where our teaching overlaps and compliments the teaching of our Chinese colleagues. We should be touching on grammar when we teach Oral English. It is certainly important, and relevant. We should consider this fact when scoring on a test. We do want students to be able to form their sentences properly, and that is grammar. When we speak of grammar in Oral English, we mean to be able to form proper simple sentences and complex sentences with appropriate conjunctions. This is not to imply that perfect grammar in every sense is required, but the goal in particular is structuring the sentence so it sounds complete and leaves the correct impression on the hearer. Students must learn to include more than just nouns and verbs in their speech.

How comfortable is the student with English? Articulation is a flow of speech that reflects the student's actual command of English. Does the student easily speak in English, or is he stammering and struggling for words? A lot of hesitation will bring the score down. Good articulation and handling words easily will bring it up.

There is no value to a vocabulary score in a speech competition because the speech is prepared and words can be memorized and found in a dictionary and placed in the speech. The student taking an exam can only use words he can apply from memory, his actual vocabulary, so we grade vocabulary and the skill of structuring sentences under articulation in an oral exam.

(Note: The Chinese student thinks in Chinese, his native language. When he speaks English, his mind is going through a translation process. He is translating his Chinese thoughts into English words. This will necessarily affect his ability to be fluent and articulate, but as he becomes more familiar with the second language he will start thinking in that second language as well

as he can think in his first language. That point of achievement is reached only after a very prolonged familiarity with the second language. This can be illustrated in a person who has emigrated from his native China to an English-speaking country. After some years in the new country he may start losing his first language and be able to speak the second language better than the first language, especially if he is separated from a Chinese community.)

4. Conversancy: Conversancy is the ease with which the student can carry on a two-way dialogue with an English person. This skill is worth 2 points. Good communication takes pronunciation and vocabulary, but probably the third most important quality is the student's ability to structure the English words into sentences that are easily understood by an English speaking person. To be conversant in English is, as mentioned above, the ultimate goal of learning a second language. It is how well the student does in holding a *two-way* conversation between himself and an English speaking person that finally reveals his comprehension. Does he understand what I am saying to him? To understand what he hears and then be able to intelligibly respond is a sign of progress in mastering your second language. It takes two or more people to converse, or communicate. When I have a conversation with my student at exam time – or any time – how smoothly does our conversation go? The more smoothly it goes, the better the score.

5. Expression: Facial expression, voice inflection, and eye contact are important parts of communication, but a student's personality may not allow him or her to be expressive. So 1 point is enough to score expression in the total CLS or a speech competition score. I will give an average student a score of 0.6 on this speech skill if he or she makes eye contact with me, but if the student looks down and mutters in an expressionless manner, he or she will get a 0.2. That could lower a total score noticeably. Some students who have come from certain backgrounds have a quality of shyness that just will not let them speak assertively or raise their voice. I am not too hard on these timid students because I see this as rather refreshing in contrast to the incontinency that has become prevalent with so many young people in recent times. I must grade them, but I warn my students that they must speak out in the exam, and I try to encourage them to speak clearly for the best grade. When the student adds facial expression and hand gestures, any kind of body language to emphasize the story, that's expression, and it will definitely improve her score. Expression includes:

1. Clarity and eye contact

2. Face and body language, and especially

3. Voice inflection.

Show me by the tone of your voice that you understand and really believe what you're talking about and that what you're telling me has eclipsed the fact that you're taking an exam (or giving a speech). It's giving your words feeling that will give you credibility with the hearer.

On the last column of the score sheet at the far right side you will have the *total*. In this column you will enter the total of the five scores which becomes his/her CLS (or speech competition) composite score.

See *Figure 16.1* on the following page for an example of typical ECLS scoring for two freshman students.

Figure 16.1

Comprehension Exam Sheet

(10 points possible)

Student	Originality 1 point	Pronunciation 3 points	Articulation 3 points	Conversancy 2 points	Expression 1 point	Total Score
Maria	0.7	2.3	1.5	1.2	0.8	6.5
Jason	0.2	1.4	0.9	1.4	0.4	4.3

[end table]

Maria: She is smiling and greets me pleasantly. Total score: 6.5 (A high score for a freshman college student.)

Jason: He is quiet and appears shy, not looking me in the eye. Total score: 4.3 (A low score for a freshman college student.)

Remember, there are two definitions for articulation. One is to pronounce a word distinctly, while it also means the ability to express meaning with words. I make a distinction between articulation and pronunciation. As mentioned above, pronunciation is the correct pronunciation of a word or words. Articulation is the ability to express oneself through a good choice and combination of words.

The occasion of this scoring is the ECLS (Entrance Comprehension Level Score) and not a graded exam. These are new students coming to college as freshmen, but when I give these students an oral exam, I will use these same five skills to grade their comprehension level.

In these two examples we first have Maria, whose mother teaches English in middle school. She is one of my high comprehenders. Note that Jason is a low comprehender in many ways, but Jason scored higher in conversancy than Maria! Why? Maria was more outgoing, but she asked me to repeat what I said once or twice. Jason always understood what I said and responded accordingly. He did not have Maria's vocabulary, but he used his smaller vocabulary well and apparently understood better than he could speak. I assumed he was a little intimidated by having to speak with the foreign teacher. This is one of the typically interesting things about scoring comprehension of students. An LC student may score higher than an HC in a certain skill. You won't notice this sometimes until after you have taken the exam sheet home and started analyzing it. You will discover many interesting things like this about your students' speech skills in the process of grading oral exams.

It's beneficial to go over the speech skills on the score sheet with the class each time you give an oral exam, explaining to the students the nature of the exam and upon what criteria they will be evaluated. Notify them in advance, so they know in which direction to concentrate their study efforts.

You may have to adjust the scores in the ECLS to arrive at a true evaluation of skill level. Note that I am referring to the *entry* oral exam given at the beginning of the term. Here you want to establish an accurate baseline. The scores for graded oral exams, given later in the semester, are never adjusted. Students will be nervous or have other legitimate dysfunctional reasons for not performing well in an ECLS. Some of them may be shy or intimidated to be standing before a foreign teacher for the first time in their lives. They may be suffering from lack of sleep or even an illness. For this reason, I like to encounter students outside the classroom on occasion and engage them in some small talk. If those casual talks impress me as being quite comprehensive and better than the ECLS I gave them, I go to the ECLS sheet and check their score. If it's considerably lower than my conversation with them indicates, I may modify the score so I have what I believe to be a more accurate evaluation of that student's comprehension. Remember, the ECLS is not a grade; it is only a comprehension score upon entering the class to be used as a reference, so I am free to modify it any time I believe it needs to be adjusted.

When I make up my comprehension sheets, I place the student's names down the left side of the sheet making the space big enough for both the Chinese and the English name of the student. The five elements of comprehension run across the top. As individual students appear before me for the oral test, I always smile and greet them cordially by name and ask them questions they can easily understand. As they speak to me in response to my question, I evaluate their speech skills under each of the elements across the top of the exam sheet, as in the example provide above for Maria and Jason.

When you grade oral exams, if you analyze your scoring, you will notice the phenomenon of mixed skills. You will discover strengths in students you hitherto considered only weak, and you will discover weaknesses in your strongest students. The comprehension exam often reveals that a student with a low score may flare in just one skill area as we saw with Jason above. I have one low scoring student right now who has a tremendous vocabulary and understands as much as or more than what I say as compared to my best comprehenders. I have several who have limited vocabulary but show excellent pronunciation skills! On the other hand, you may have good students with good vocabularies and good comprehension, but when conversing with them, you can hardly understand them because their pronunciation is so bad! I always have several students in this category. I give them a lot of attention, taking them aside to discuss their problem with them privately. If I succeed at improving their pronunciation, I will have top-level students, but until they get their pronunciation improved, their other skills will be depreciated by the poor pronunciation factor.

Oral testing is intended to determine students' progress in speech skills in the five categories we covered above. There is no composition, no memorization, and no preparation for the oral exam. In fact, I take great care to make the oral exam as extemporaneous for the students as possible. This way the students have no idea what they are going to be talking about with me. I announce the exam time, of course, but what they are going to talk about with me, they have no idea. By doing this you are able to accurately measure the students' actual speech skills. I may give a review covering material that will include items to be found in the exam but nothing specific that will trigger their tendency to memorize.

For a teacher used to giving only written exams, the oral exam could be a little intimidating. It might seem to require a great deal of time, concentration, and subjective evaluation. However, once you have practiced this method of speech skill, you will easily adjust. Here are some tips on the process to make it easier. Note that these tips apply primarily to the exam desk mode of oral examination:

Get Ready, Get Set, GO!

When you plan for the exam, you must consider the timing. Let's take a reading pronunciation exam for example. A class of 32 can be examined with a twelve line printed paragraph within the two hours of (college level) class time if you have your class organized and ready to go.

When setting up an oral exam, a small desk set up with a chair or stool on either side in the front of the room will suffice. The teacher sits opposite the student being tested. I allow the class to talk in a hushed tone. If I have the class in a large room, I have the students sit in the rear of the classroom and take the exam in the front of the room. As soon as students finish their exam with me, they must pass out of the room to another designated room and wait until I come and dismiss the class. I usually like to discuss the scores and a general impression I have from the exam if the time permits. If not, I cover it in the next class. They like this comment from the teacher, and I sometimes mention some students who have made marked progress in the scoring.

You should begin with a brief instruction about how the exam will be taken and a reminder to be prompt getting to the exam table. I have my class monitor and class secretaries help me to line up the students as they appear on my roster. This makes for easier movement to the test chair. As I test one student, I have the next three to five students come and stand in line ready to move quickly into the test chair, but always just outside of hearing distance. I put the monitor in charge of keeping them in line and ready.

I read the exam paragraph once to individual students to make them slightly familiar with the test text, but I make no comments. There is an average of ten words per line, which means the exam paragraph(s) will total about 100 to 120 words. On a reading exam this gives you ample time to take a score. Your early scoring experiences will take a little longer, but after a few oral exams this timing is about standard. If you are giving a full 5 skill comprehension score (grade), then 12 lines will give you the extra time you need to more accurately evaluate the student's speech skills.

If you print the exam paragraph(s) on your computer printer, it's better that you print it at 14 to 16 point font size and double-space the lines. This makes it easier for the student to read.

I tell students their grade after I have scored the exam. If they are doing below average, I encourage them to study more and try harder. If they do well, I commend them with some words of encouragement. Some teachers have slips prepared and write the student's score on the slip and hand it to the student as he or she leaves the exam table. That's a good idea. Students are intense at exam time and very interested in their grades. No matter how well they do, they will always say they should have done better. I keep all grade records in files for several years in case I need to refer to them.

Sometimes if a student makes a very high score or shows extremely good progress, which indicates she has been diligently studying and practicing her oral English, I may tell her the improvement in her last two or three scores to encourage her. If a student had a particular difficulty during the exam, I always try to quickly go over the words she had trouble with and tell her where she needs to apply more study to overcome her problem. After the exams are finished, I go over the score sheet with the class, explaining to everyone the weaknesses that showed up on that particular exam as well as noticeable improvements. If there is an outstanding achievement, especially by an LC student, I will mention his or her name and let the class know about the impressive performance. This is a great encouragement to that student who may have given up hope, and it improves his standing in the eyes of his classmates. It also encourages the class, demonstrating that hard work does pay off! In short, I note the scoring trend of the whole class as compared to their previous performances. I will read scores that climbed from the last exam and note features of their scoring that pleased me. I say everything I possibly can that's positive and encouraging to them. When I make this review of scores, I never mention names unless it is in congratulations!

In creating the exam, I always find it beneficial to *stretch the mind a little.* I try to include three to four words that I am sure are new words such as *waist, splashing,* or *muddy,* words that are common but not used that much in our class studies. It is good to see how they handle the process of sounding out their syllables as they tackle a new word. I have taught them how to do this, and this tells me if they have been working on syllables. I have been pressing them in almost every class. *"Sound out the syllables!" "How many syllables?" "How many vowels?"* Many students, to my delight, have surprised me by handling new words like pros! When they do that, a couple of tenths of a point are added to the pronunciation score. Any show of skill in handling the language means points in an oral exam.

Chapter Seventeen
Scoring Methods for the Oral Exam

Oral exam grading really is more taxing than giving a written exam, but it can also be more enjoyable as you get to converse with students, get a sense of their true ability, and often get to be surprised by them. However, you must develop a capacity to do good scoring at the exam table.

Remember that when you are giving the ECLS, you are not assigning a grade. This is only a score taken at the beginning of the school year to let the teacher know each student's comprehension level upon entering the class. This is a different matter than scoring a student in the oral exam. This is the score that we give when testing the student's oral progress, and it is the score that will make up the student's semester grade when totaled. Please note the difference between the term, *grading* and the term, *scoring.* We must not confuse these two terms. A grade and a score are sometimes two different things. A grade is determined by scores on an exam, but a score is not always a grade, as in the ECLS. When giving a score that will constitute a grade, this is a matter of importance to the student, and that score must be as accurate and carefully taken as possible.

A Quick Comprehension Level – CL – Scoring Method:

This is a quick and quite accurate way to establish a CL. First you determine which level out of 10 a student's performance places him in, and place him in a level of the 40's, 50's, or the 60's, or even 70's. Once you have placed him on the level of 10 in which he belongs, then you must determine the level at which he is performing, between a one and a nine. If you place this student in the 50's, then you listen carefully to place his level of speech somewhere between 51 and 59.

I have had only one senior student in my years of teaching in China who was in the 80's, the high 80's! She was the exception. She came from the countryside and was endowed with a brilliant mind. I often thought of how unfortunate it would have been if she had not had the opportunity to receive a formal education, as many brilliant and gifted young people from the countryside do not.

Starting in the 40's, I will help you find the right 10 slots for your student. This student before me does quite well handling the language but is struggling and halting before releasing some words. This student can carry on a quite good but strained conversation with me, and his pronunciation is far from perfect. I place him in the 50's because he is conversant and understands me quite well when I question him. Next, I will grade him somewhere between 50 and 60. In his speech, he handles a couple of words very well and uses a couple of adjectives cleverly. This will give him a grade several points above 50, but he pronounces his –*l's* poorly (one of the most difficult tasks for the Chinese mouth), so I score him in the mid 50's.

I continue to listen carefully to place his final score either below or above the mid 50's. I fail to understand several of his words, so I decide to give him .4 above his 50. His final score is 5.4.

Keep in mind we are talking here about a comprehension score and **not** an exam score. This is not the method you use for giving oral exams when starting out. We will treat that later.

After you have become proficient at comprehension scoring, you can use this method for grading, but doing your entry scores in which no grades are involved is a good time to use this method of scoring for practice. On your first oral exams that determine a student's grade, you should carefully grade on the five speech skills until you become proficient in scoring on the *Quick Ten Method.*

Here are some guidelines for placing students in the appropriate ten slot:

40: Very poor comprehension and speech skills. He struggles to speak (incorrectly) and is hardly intelligible. I begin with 40 as the lowest possible speech performance for a college freshman. With these *special* students, we must smile and thank them for their performance and assure them that *"That's fine."* Many of these bad impressions on the entry CLS turn out to be hard workers and high achievers with a little encouragement. They surprise me many times. I sometimes meet very low comprehenders off campus, and they shock the daylights out of me wanting to talk my leg off! Also, they may be very nervous if they are shy, but after they get to know you they are much better comprehenders than their ECLS indicated. At any rate, students who rate in the 40s will have demonstrated very little two-way comprehension, and may answer your question inappropriately based upon misunderstanding.

50's: Poor expression and low vocabulary, struggle with their words but show some two-way comprehension. They are markedly better than those in the 40's, but speak very broken English. They seem to understand my question, sometimes asking me to repeat it. I always accommodate their request graciously, but if they just can't understand what I am saying, I smile and give a word of assurance and tell them I have their score and that they will do better as they follow me in class and study hard. The 50's are a ten above the 40's. The class average, determined by adding the total scores of all students, divided by the number of students, in an entry oral – ECLS – is going to be between 50 and 55, if your grading is about right. My averages have always been around 5.3 for freshmen classes. Anything above 5.5 is above average, and with this figure you can determine where to place your students' skill level between the 40's up into the 60's. You will usually have several who come to college with their English in the 60's. Next you must decide if this student in the 40's is closer to a low 40 or showed a high 40 toward 50. The same is true with the student who scores in the 60's. Was she closer to a 70 or in the low 60's? As I listen to each student I determine if she is having some serious problems with using the right words and place her in the low 60's. I may give her a 6.3.

60's: Now we get to the better comprehenders. The 60's are comprehenders and their conversing skill is quite good, especially in the high 60's. Your exchanges go off well, but maybe a little slow, or show a small vocabulary. These students are usually more relaxed and more confident talking to you. They may speak a bit slowly, have pronunciation that is a bit off, and leave out a few conjunctions or prepositions, but you can understand them quite well. The 60's need improvement, but we are conversing with very little strain.

70's: These students are speaking as well as the average senior student and are starting to think in English. Their comprehension is quite good, and there are no really big problems in their speech. They may have some poor pronunciation but not much. They can put a sentence together well and understand everything you say if you speak clearly. These students are working more on vocabulary now than on comprehension. Scoring in the 70's is a high achievement for all college level students. The highest score I have encountered in a senior has been an 8.4, as previously mentioned.

80's: Very few pre-grad students ever reach an 8.0 in spoken English. The 80's and higher are usually the post grad levels of English majors who have mastered their second language and have frequently spent time abroad in an English-speaking country. These are also beginning to think in English when speaking English.

90's: These achievers are now thinking in English as well as Chinese without having to translate anything in their minds before speaking. English is almost as natural to them as their native Chinese tongue. Usually these achievers have also lived abroad in an English speaking culture.

After you have heard each student speak, you will have a very good idea of your class comprehension skills. That information will help you know where to start and what level of teaching they need. You will begin to feel the challenge and start biting at the bit to bring up their speech level. For example, let us say a new teacher fresh from the States has arrived on campus and is looking forward to her first classes with freshmen. She is going to have a total of 212 students in her 16 hours of classes each week. She has read this manual and decided to give the ECLS to each of her freshman students. New teachers are especially smart to do this because they can get some good experience giving comprehension scores knowing it's not going to affect the students' grades. So, she will practice giving orals to 212 students in a week's time! After giving 212 orals, she has accrued enough experience to make her much more comfortable when she has to give her first exams that will become the all-important grade.

After some experience giving oral exams, you will be able to give scores by using the Quick Ten Method of scoring and know quite accurately a person's CL by listening a short time to him or her. You will be doing what I do when I talk to any new Chinese friends who speak English. I am scoring their English skills while we're talking, unbeknownst to them. I simply do it out of habit. Oral scoring is essentially a subjective method, but this is not necessarily a weakness. Even though the score is totally determined by the teacher's own listening skills, there are plenty of ways the teacher can prove the accuracy of her scoring. You will find it interesting and fun, and above all, *The proof is in the puddin'* when we show you how you can prove your accuracy in giving oral scores in this next chapter.

Chapter Eighteen
Double-checking the Accuracy of Your Oral Scoring

While your evaluation of student speech skills during the interview is somewhat subjective, there are several ways to double-check the accuracy of your scores. Checking your accuracy helps you to feel assured that you are assigning fair and useful grades, and it also helps you to fine-tune your scoring methods, if you determine that your scores seem a little off.

Self-Evaluation

One of the best ways to test the accuracy of your scoring is through what I call the student's self-evaluation comprehension score. For this exercise you must first hand out to every student a quarter-sized sheet of paper – one-fourth of a standard stationery sheet. Tell students to write their name and class number and date at the top of the paper. When they have finished doing that, you have them lay the paper on their desk upside down with nothing in their hands and listen carefully as you read. The item you read should be a little over their heads. It should be about five to ten minutes long. A business news item or other news story or short story is good material for this. Read carefully and slowly with good clear diction. Your goal is to be sure they hear and understand as much of the article as possible, even though you know they are not going to understand all of it.

When you have finished reading, you explain to them that you want them to mark on the paper you gave them, the percentage of the article they understood. I take the time to go over what percentage means and illustrate it on the board. As always, before they write anything on the paper, they must understand perfectly what you're asking them to do. Explain that 50% means they understood about half of what you read. If they understood less than half, have them write 40 or 45%. If they understood more than half, 60% or even 70%, then they are to write that percentage they understood on the paper. They are not to look on each other's papers but put down a figure that reflects their own comprehension only! Encourage them to think carefully before writing their figure on the paper. If they feel they understood 65%, then put that down.

In this self-evaluation of individual comprehension, you will also discover the honesty of the Chinese student. I have conducted this activity many times and have never once known a student to inflate his or her self-evaluation.

When you gather these papers, you will then compare the student's self-evaluation with your scoring on the CLS sheet you have filled out. You will likely find an amazing parallel between the scores you gave students and their own evaluations! When I had the idea to do this with my students, the first time I was stunned by the fact that, with very few exceptions, their self-evaluation figures matched the ECLS I gave them, or the scores I gave them on oral exams. Often the uneven score they gave to themselves, such as 67%, actually was that student's score on the last oral exam I gave (6.7)! There were very few exceptions to this parallel between their self-evaluation and my CLS. This exercise demonstrates the honesty of the student and the honesty of and impartial scoring by the teacher. Try it sometime. If you give this test to your class and their scores do not match your scores, it may be that they did not fully understand your instructions. Try the exercise again, this time making absolutely sure they understand what you are asking them to do. If they understand, listen carefully, and write down their own comprehension of what was read, you will most likely see the parallel.

The Word Hunt

After you have done the year's first scoring of students entering the class, calculate the non-graded score. A good way to test the accuracy of your scoring is to have a word hunt. I will repeat the instructions for this exercise for your convenience, though they are the same if you are using the word hunt as a learning exercise or as a way to test scoring accuracy. The word hunt can actually accomplish both purposes at once! First, hand out a quarter-sized sheet of paper to every student. Write a long English word of your choice on the blackboard. (I used the example of the word *extemporaneously* in my previous mention of this exercise.) Have each student write the word across the top of his paper under his name, class number, and date.

Now you will discuss the word and its meaning with the class. It's a word they will not use much but nevertheless an interesting word for an oral English class discussion and this word hunt to test their vocabulary *and your scoring*.

You must explain the rules clearly. We want to see how many words can be found in the word written on the board, in this case, *extemporaneously*. Students can only use the letters in the word to make other words. They cannot use a letter more times than it is found in the word. For example, the word *extreme* is valid because there are three –*e's* in the word, but the word *support* is not valid because there is only one *–p* in *extemporaneously*. After explaining the rules, give them 20 to 30 minutes to find as many words as possible in that word, using only the letters in the word. Instruct them to number their words. This will help you when you check how many words each student was able to list.

Let me tell you the results I had in two freshmen classes. The average number of words listed on each student's sheet was between 25 and 38 words. Now there are several things you can do with these word lists. First, I compare the English vocabulary of each student, taking the number of words they have each listed and comparing that number with their ECLS. You will see that the number of words they were able to find will parallel the score you gave them on your ECLS. Sometimes the parallel is uncanny. For example, if a student made a low 4.3 (43) on his ECLS putting him at the bottom of the class, his vocabulary power will usually correspond to where he is on the class score you gave him on their entry comprehension score. In this way you are again assured that your scoring is hitting the mark. However, there will be deviations when you have exceptional students.

You will be shocked by how well some LC's do on this vocabulary test! It's a lesson for the teacher. One boy I had in my class was rated by the English department as a slow learner, having a difficult time especially with his pronunciation, but he made a score of 70 words taken from the search word! He scored above all of my HC's and amazed me. I had noted his vocabulary was good but did not realize it was *that* good. The word hunt gave me a good opportunity to commend him before the class and give him the encouragement he needed. He was definitely the vocabulary king in my four classes! Those are some of the interesting things we find in giving such exercises. A high score by an LC does not disprove the correlation between your scoring and the student scores but proves that we do have some students with exceptional skills who may flare in one of the skills even though their average scores in all of the five speech skills scored together are low.

An additional step you can take with the word hunt is to appoint the class secretaries to add up the total number of words found by all members of the class collectively. They were amazed, and I was too, to find that all four classes combined found a total of 323 words in the word *extemporaneously*! If you do this exercise with several classes, you can have a competition between them. When I do this, I don't announce any totals until all totals are in. The competition gets pretty intense. It is fun, and it serves several purposes, including giving me a way to check my scoring and developing the English language skills of the students. An activity is best when it produces multiple benefits.

Speech Competitions

Sometimes you will be invited to judge a speech competition. This can be an excellent way to improve your scoring accuracy. I have often sat on a panel of six to eight judges scoring student speech competitions. After each student finishes, the scores of the judges are gathered, and the score of each student is announced. The amazing thing about the scores being announced was that they were always within a point or two of the score I gave, and that was the average of all the judges! This indicates that the judges, including myself, were all giving about the same score to that student. Students I scored high, the rest of the judges had scored high. Students I scored low, they had scored low as well. In one instance, the total score of a student was precisely the score I gave to that student! When the five skills of an oral sheet are being scored by experienced English teachers, the scores tend to average about the same by each judge. This should give us confidence that we are providing fair and accurate evaluations of our students' skills. (Remember, however, the five skills we use to score a student taking an extemporaneous exam in class, are different than the skills we list in a speech competition, but you will find the accuracy of your assessment is not affected by this difference in emphasis.)

Written Exams

Another way to double-check your scoring is to take a look at the scores and grades the students are making on their written exams as a point of comparison. I sometimes give one written exam a school year to emphasize the importance of taking notes and listening to the Talk Along lectures that usually deal with important life issues. Knowing they're going to face an exam tends to perk them up and causes them to pay more attention to the subject material. For example, I will often give a written exam on the content material after having done a series of oral sessions and discussions on topics such as joint ventures or foreign trade agreements. You will usually find that the scores of the students on the written exam will correspond with the scores you've given them on their CL's. Even though one is written and the other is oral, there will still be a useful point of comparison. As noted in the word hunt, however, be prepared for surprises.

These exercises don't give you a foolproof mode of affirming your scoring accuracy, but taken together, they give you an opportunity to explore your scoring practices and arrive at a comfortable conclusion. Through experience and the continual inquiry that these accuracy checks provide, you should feel confident in your scoring in no time!

Chapter Nineteen
Teaching Resources and Class Materials

You will either use materials provided by the school, you may develop your own class curricula, or you could mix them, depending on the policy of the school for which you are teaching. I have used all of these methods in different schools.

For example, I have:

1. Used a workbook and manuals with a teaching plan built in;

2. Compiled my own materials (readers, news events, short novels, and other good material for reading and discussion) and developed my own teaching plan;

3. Built my own class teaching plan using the school's English manuals.

Each of these options has its advantages.

The workbook contains stories usually followed by many different kinds of word study exercises on the pages following the story. This is a good way to cover a certain amount of territory within a planned time frame of a semester. It is also a good guide to follow by new teachers who may need help in having a teaching plan. Workbooks are excellent for achieving a systematic goal or learning level in the duration of a school term or semester. Workbooks are not only important for the student, but also for the teacher. Some workbooks suit the teacher's preferences more than others. You should consult your dean to preview the workbook(s) the school has been using. You may ask him or her to allow you to choose your own workbook that better fits your particular skills and style of teaching. If you discuss it with the department colleagues before they have made a purchase, they will usually agree to this. You should look over the many workbooks available in bookstores and become familiar with them for future use in your classes. This is another good reason for arriving on the job some days before classes begin. You need to look over the different workbooks and be sure they are story-centered workbooks that provoke good discussion, something essential to teaching Oral English. There are some workbooks that are good for teaching grammar, composition and writing, but you will want the workbook that features stories. Look for one with large, clear print and exercises following the story theme. You can then add any new twist you like to the material in each story lesson.

The alternative to using a workbook is to compile your own materials, perhaps ones that you have collected over years of teaching. A reader is essential for Read Along exercises. The text should develop the vocabulary and provoke a discussion. Compiling your own materials is a method most often used by teachers who have been teaching in China for several years and have developed their own subject material and teaching methods they feel are effective. This method will include reading stories with the class – Read Along – to accomplish your own goals. I am personally comfortable with either method. I teach a business English course, which I devised, that familiarizes students with business vocabulary and basic enterprise principles that will serve them very well as they enter the real world of business after their graduation. I use an enterprise economics chart I designed to hand out to the students. Some teachers have several subjects and theme studies they have compiled and use for class material. It may be random, but if the teacher is skilled, it can be very effective to have a variety of subjects you can treat.

Study Materials

Good, professional study materials place the greatest importance on common words and phrases. I can recommend the Oxford Picture Dictionary studies which can be found at http://www.picturedictionary.org.

You might also search for the Oxford University Press. The Chinese-English list of books, manuals and the overhead loose-leaf transparency binder are all excellent tools for teaching the common English nouns and verbs. It's a little expensive but extremely well done and useful if you have a teaching environment that can accommodate an overhead projector. If not, you can copy the pages and use them as handouts. The two items you will most definitely want are the *Oxford Picture Dictionary* and the *Classroom Activities Manual* for the Teacher. Don't look at the price because you will not be disappointed when you get these books in your hands.

The British Broadcasting Corporation – BBC – in cooperation with Longman's Publishing puts out an excellent set of Chinese/English teacher's manuals and workbooks that rate right up there with the Oxford materials. You can find them on the web by searching, *Look Ahead Classroom Course,* but there are many manuals and workbooks available in the Chinese bookstores that are almost identical in content and format.

Then after you arrive in China, there are also some very good materials titled *Up Close* that you can get at a very reasonable price right here. These are wonderfully formatted in color with oodles of classroom methods and ideas for teaching an Oral English class. You can check them out by visiting www.fltrp.com.cn and then http://upclose.heinle.com also. They print several levels. I have the Number 1 and the Number 2 volumes. They are large and colorful and full of teaching ideas. All workbooks you will find have classroom activities and discussion materials. As I mentioned in the beginning of this manual, the *Oral Workshop: Discussion,* distributed by the Foreign Language Teaching and Research Press, is a very good reader for Read Along exercises. This manual will have material for just about any style of teaching preference.

The book, *The Spirit of the Chinese People,* is recommended reading for any new teacher coming to China. It was written by a Chinese gentleman, Ku Hung-Ming, in 1915 during a time of great turmoil in China. If you want to better understand the peculiar and mild temperament of the Chinese, read this book.

Usually the school for which you are working has its own standard teaching materials, but if you have a reader or manual you would like to recommend, your administrators will examine it and usually approve it and provide it for your classes. I like the *Oral Workshop: Discussion* reader mentioned above and requested it for my classes. It was approved and provided by the college. If a workbook or reader meets the academic standard of the college examiners, they will usually be happy to provide it. Let me make a comment here concerning teaching materials that may be handed to you by the college. I have gently explained to my superiors that I prefer not to use workbooks in my class because they are used in the English classes taught by the Chinese teachers. I explain carefully that my preference is a good reader and then have it with me and break it out for them to look at. It has always been acceptable. I further explain that I place a greater emphasis on spoken English by using a reader in my classes. Those in authority always respect that explanation and usually allow you latitude in choosing your material when they believe you know what you're talking about. They want you to feel comfortable with your teaching job, and they will carefully look over any material you show them to determine whether or not it meets their standards.

Sometimes the college FAO office will provide you with an English workbook that teaches grammar, but as I emphasize strongly in this manual, Oral English teachers are called here to teach spoken English – not to duplicate grammar lessons the Chinese teachers are teaching in their English classes. Remember our primary mission is to give the Chinese student something the Chinese teachers cannot give them – pure native spoken English! Everything we do in our classes should provide the student with the opportunity to hear and speak English with the foreign teacher. This is what the student longs for and what the national education leaders in Beijing expect us to give them.

One tool the teacher can use constantly for many purposes is a good Chinese/English *talking* dictionary that can talk in Chinese as well as English. There are many electronic dictionaries in large and small shops in any town. They are everywhere here in China because English is so popular. Most of these are programmed to help the Chinese speaking person. If you, as a teacher, want a dictionary that accommodates the English-speaking person, then you will have to get that from the English-speaking country from which you are coming.

I searched literally for years to find the ideal translator with English and Chinese voices and finally found it! I hope to save you the time and energy, to say nothing of not having the tool so many times when you badly need it. I can point you directly to the best and only such tool I know. On the Internet go to http://www.ectaco.com and enjoy yourself. I have the model EC5900HV. It is just amazingly easy to use and absolutely the best thing I have had to help me here in China. It will help you in your classroom teaching to learn Chinese yourself, and when traveling and doing your shopping, it's the next best thing to having an interpreter with you! I use it constantly in the classroom in many ways when teaching new words. My students are intrigued by it. The cost is about $250 but worth it if you can make that investment in a good teaching tool. If you do not have access to a computer, you may write to them at:

Ectaco Corporate Center
31-21 31st Street,
Long Island City,
NY, 11106

If You Want to Learn Chinese

If you are interested in learning the Chinese language, there are many books and taped programs in all of the Chinese bookstores here in China you can visit after you arrive. If they don't have it in the small city where you work, they will have a larger selection in a nearby capital city. Bookstores are everywhere. You can go to a bookstore with an interpreter and buy children's Pinyin language books that give you a good start in learning Pinyin pronunciation with illustrations, at a very low price. Every bookstore will have large English sections where you can find a wide selection of manuals, textbooks, and workbooks to fit your teaching needs. There is also a good deal of Chinese language software available on the Internet. Try contacting www.transparent.com and look up their *Chinese Now* software program.

Informational Websites

There are also websites that can give you a great deal of general information about becoming a foreign teacher. Probably one of the best sites for teachers, who are contemplating teaching in China, or are already teaching in China is: http://overseasdigest.com/schooljobs.htm.

You will learn a whole lot about the English language industry on this site and also by visiting www.tealic.com. They cover the gamut in all aspects of the China scene for teachers. There are forums here, for example, where you can log on and ask experienced teachers in China your questions. These and other sites will fill you in on information too extensive to add to this condensed manual.

Audiotapes

Tapes play a very important part in teaching English to the Chinese student. There is a definite place for audiotapes in teaching Oral English, especially for the Chinese teacher of English who wants to give the students varied exposure to the sound of native English. Playing an audiotape and then discussing the subject is a good exercise, but more effective is any exercise that uses a text for the student to Read Along with the English-speaking teacher. By this they see and hear the pure English, and their dreams of speaking with a foreign teacher are being fulfilled. They are seeing and hearing it pronounced, making a correct double mental impression. Most programs such as those put out by Oxford and BBC include tapes as a vital part of their product-line.

I must repeat this point in a different way: Learning English is best accomplished when the *student* is speaking English. That is what we have to get the student to do, to speak English *with us*. But, not just to talk or speak English as they know it, but to speak it correctly with someone they know, who knows the language well! Knowing the correct sound of each word they speak and how to use that word meaningfully in a sentence is the goal of both teacher and student.

Chapter Twenty
Living in China

Cost of Living

At the time of this writing, the Chinese currency, known as RMB or yuan, is a pegged currency, meaning that the value is set by the Chinese government. In recent years, the currency has been losing its value against the dollar as China attempts to value their currency more equally with the international floating currencies. At this writing we can say that the cost of living in China is getting higher for the Chinese people, and especially the poor, as consumer goods are fast approaching the costs of goods in the United States with the exception of a few items. Products made outside of China will cost more. Your cost of living at this writing will be about the same as in the States with the exception of a few items such as haircuts and food sold in the smaller restaurants. Depending on your lifestyle, the cost will be about the same over a month's expenses. Your utilities and rent are provided by the school. It also depends on the city you're living in.

The cost of living is lower in smaller towns than in the large Eastern seacoast industrialized cities. But the cost of living in China will still be noticeably less than in Europe, in comparison. A bus fare is very cheap at about 15 cents in most cities compared to transportation in the West. The pay for foreign teachers is higher in the coastal cities where the cost of living is higher – sometimes twice as high as inland universities and schools.

The salary they pay foreign teachers is two to three times what the Chinese teachers are paid IN A MIDDLE SCHOOL, and many of them have families, and they all manage to save money! So we foreign teachers fare well compared to our Chinese peers.

Markets

Outdoor markets are everywhere! The fresh fruits and vegetables are prolific. The South of China produces and ships to the Northern cities many exotic fruits including pineapple, kiwi, oranges, dates, lemons, and many other fruits with which most Westerners are not even familiar. Some markets are not as nice as others, but there are many so you can find the better ones easily. The price of vegetables and fruits is ridiculously low compared to the West, but you should be careful to wash or peel everything carefully.

Food markets and private grocery stores are not far from wherever you may live. Pork is the big meat staple in China, followed by lamb and chicken, but beef is available in the bigger supermarkets or in the special Muslim meat shops. These specialize in beef: shaved beef and beef roasts. Beef hotdogs are hard to come by.

If you see something you like on a store shelf, you'd better buy a whole box or several dozen because you may not see it again for 6 to 8 months, or ever! The shop buyers have not yet learned the art of strategic restocking. They do not always keep their shelves stocked with the high sellers, so when it's gone, it's gone and you may never see it again. *Get it while the gettin's good!*

Restaurants

If you are not in the habit of doing your own cooking, you should have nothing to worry about. There are ten thousand restaurants lining the streets of every sizeable Chinese city! Remember, though, that you are in the heartland of hot and spicy food in Central and North-Central China. Chongqing is the "hotpot city," famous for very spicy, hot foods. I have lived in China for years, and I still see new dishes of Chinese food every time I walk into a restaurant. Even if you do cook for yourself, you can afford to have a three-course meal at a decent restaurant for as little as 20 yuan – less than three dollars. The best meal in the finest restaurant can be had for six to seven dollars, and it's plenty for two people to eat. If it's anniversary time or you want to splurge, you can usually find a five star hotel with a buffet that's exquisite and will cost you 10 to 12 USD.

You can order several good noodle dishes for 2 to 3 yuan in very good restaurants. I prefer Jiajiang mein noodles because they are not soupy, containing the city water. It's more of a fried noodle topped with vegetables and a tasty meat sauce. It usually costs between 2 to 3 yuan – 25 to 35 cents USD. One small bowl is enough for two people, but a large bowl is *plenty* for two!

Sidewalk eateries are everywhere, and you can have a big *bing* vegetable sandwich which includes a fried egg for 1 yuan – about 15 to 20 cents USD, but be careful to eat only at the clean places. Don't let your joy at the sight of a bargain – 20 cents for a great full-meal sandwich – overwhelm your good judgment. An American teacher friend of mine was eating the bing vegetable sandwiches almost every day. The bing sandwich has several vegetables, tofu noodles, and a fried egg all fried together. He was four months battling acute dyspepsia – dysentery! He didn't know what was causing it until he discovered it was his 12-cent bargain lunch! These bings are delicious, but just be sure the seller is clean or buy the bing bread and make them yourself at home.

Water is often tainted with chlorine and other chemicals, but you can get pure, robust water delivered to your door very inexpensively. I found a restaurant that had the bottles of pure water in each eating room. Needless to say, when I visit Hui Xian, I always eat there. Hermetically sealed drinks are also everywhere. Most restaurants carry sweetened yogurt, fruit drinks, and soft drinks. My favorite is bottled green tea, but you sometimes must buy that and take it with you to the restaurant because they often do not carry the bottled tea on the menu.

The service is beyond anything you have experienced in your life. Waitresses watch over you like mother hens, and if you want a green tea, they will send after it and charge you nothing extra for the errand. Colas and Sprite, of course, are everywhere, but they also have fruit juices in cardboard containers. You can usually view the drinks in an upright glass door cooler.

Just so your palate isn't alarmed, let me warn you that Chinese soups such as egg soup, and other soups appearing to be salty, are often sweet in China. They put sugar in soups, breads, and other foods that we do not in the West. Many Western snacks that appear on the shelves here are also sweetened or have spicy hot added to Chinese-ize them to the local taste. Pringles potato chips are the same as they are in the West, fortunate for those of us who like a salty snack!

In China, McDonald's and KFC's are springing up all over! KFC has added a mild hot spice to the chicken batter. Pizza Hut has also invaded, along with Wal-Mart. These chains are mostly located in the larger coastal cities, but are spreading to the inland cities fast. Wal-Mart is also adding stores in the large cities. Cities like Beijing and Kunmiong have Wal-Marts now, and one will be built next year in Zhengzhou.

Transportation

I usually take a bus when traveling between cities within a hundred miles. Trains are for longer distances, but flying is by far the less congested and quicker option for long distances. To fly from North to South China will cost about 150 dollars one-way. Domestic air tickets are comparable or some lower than U.S. fares. The airports are modern and functional. The Chinese people are friendly and helpful, so you can always get around by asking or making motions. I fly frequently and travel into remote areas – Tibet, Sichuan, and I never have any problems. Planes are frequently delayed when flights do not originate at your departure point, but other than that it's not difficult. Travel agents can be found at the airports, along the street, and in large hotels. You will find an agency in the city where you teach, or you can go through the FAO office of your school, and they will help you arrange for tickets.

Technology

They do have broadband in China. Many campuses have it cabled into their buildings, readily available, but you must pay for this service. Most schools supply all utilities but provide a phone allowance of 100 to 200 yuan a month for phone service. You will pay for calls over that allowance. If you're frugal, you can easily make it on what they allow. China also has *www* computer cards, which allow you to use your computer or another person's computer on any telephone line by entering that card number to get on line. Prepaid phone cards are also available in almost any shop along the street. They have the home phone card that costs less that you can use only on your registered home phone number. The *anywhere* card costs a little more but can be used on any phone except to or from a mobile phone.

Speaking of phones, China is the number one mobile phone market in the world and almost everyone has one! It has more cell phone users than any country in the world, and the number is growing! Here, at present, there are no free cell phone offers as we have in the United States. You will pay anywhere from 900 yuan – 120 USD – to 6,000 - 8,000 yuan – 1,000 USD – for high-end cell phones with all the extras. China is now introducing the international cell phone models that will allow you to buy or bring your cell phone with you from the West and use it here by simply buying the China chip – 100 USD – when you arrive. There are three levels of service now. The first is the International chips, but they only work for one-way calling outside the country. The second level of service is the chip that covers all of China, and the third is a chip that sells in cheap phones for only a few hundred yuan that only serves the city you live in. These are inexpensive, and the call cost is very low, which many people in the large cities like. Incoming calls cost you nothing. This service is a seven-digit number, and the person you call pays nothing. I intentionally avoid giving specific details of cost here because these will change over time. You can get the current rates after you arrive in China, but I would reassure you that the cost of cell phone use is reasonable.

China is almost the same latitude as the United States. It's very warm in the South and very cold in the North in the winter! If you are familiar with the general weather patterns in the USA, then you can figure about the same for China when you come. One thing you can do to help you know what your climate will be like in the city where you're going to be teaching, is to go to the Internet to www.wunderground.com or www.weather.com and type in the name of the city at the top of the page, and either site will give you a seven or ten day weather forecast. You can see the temperatures there in both Celsius and Fahrenheit.

A Final Note

If you are thinking of coming to China to teach, I highly recommend that you approach it as a vocation and not a vacation! Experiencing this admirable culture and making many Chinese friends will be something that will give you joy for years to come. If you come here to teach, remember that you have been given an important responsibility to enrich the lives of the young people of China. See it as a serious responsibility, do your job with diligence and love, and keep your eyes and ears open because you will learn as much as those you're teaching – things that will change you forever.

Textual Initialisms and Glossary

ECLS	**Entry Comprehension Level Score** – Taken upon entry into college Oral English class
ELA	**English Latin Alphabet**
FAO	**Foreign Affairs Office**
FLD	**Foreign Language Department**
GCLS	**Graded Comprehension Level Score** – An oral exam that is a grade exam score
HC	**High Comprehender**
IELTS	**International English Language Testing System** – Test of English language proficiency
IPA	**International Phonetic Alphabet**
LC	**Low Comprehender**
PLA	**Pinyin Latin Alphabet**
RMB	**Renminbi (yuan)** – Chinese currency

CPSIA information can be obtained at www.ICGtesting.com
Printed in the USA
LVOW131700060712

289061LV00019B/197/P